"This book is a much-needed and u
psychoanalysis. M. Guy Thompson
vative works have made significant c
existentialism and psychoanalysis, but this volume is the first to integrate them. He brings his deeply personal biography and theoretical insights to bear in this uncommonly accessible work with lucid and exceptionally clear writing devoid of jargon.

Thompson's sources include Freud but also Winnicott, Bion, Lacan, Nietzsche, Heidegger and Sartre, but especially Laing, with whom he studied and worked intimately for many years in London. Thompson's conception of existential psychoanalysis is both a unique and groundbreaking contribution to the field that brings this school into the vanguard of the twenty-first century.

In our present-day technologically minded world Thompson's plea for a return of personhood, freedom, choice, genuine relationship and authenticity to the field of psychoanalysis makes this book essential reading for analysts, therapists, patients, philosophers and anyone interested in the human condition."

Emeritus Professor Douglas Kirsner, PhD, *author of* The Schizoid World of Jean-Paul Sartre and R. D. Laing

"M. Guy Thompson is a true pioneer in the field of existential psychoanalysis. In this brilliant introduction to this school, he describes in crystal clear prose the philosophical and theoretical roots of this singular approach, as well as its underpinnings in practice. In total this volume will open readers to a world of psychoanalysis they rarely access but that is likely to be critical to their growth and enrichment as humane healers."

Kirk J. Schneider, *author of* Existential-Integrative Psychotherapy and Life-Enhancing Anxiety

Existential Psychoanalysis

A fascinating introductory volume, *Existential Psychoanalysis: A Contemporary Introduction* integrates existential philosophy with psychoanalysis, drawing on key theorists from both areas and expertly guiding the reader on how to incorporate these two disciplines, which may appear disparate on the surface, into their clinical and theoretical work.

This unique and accessible book sees M. Guy Thompson explore key concepts, such as experience, authenticity, freedom, psychic change, agency, and the pervasive role of suffering in our lives. Throughout, he draws on a wide range of thinkers from both fields, including Sartre, Heidegger, Nietzsche, Freud, Winnicott, Bion, Laing, and Lacan. Exquisitely lucid and engaging, Thompson deftly brings the reader into thoughtful and enlightening territory typically inaccessible to the general reader. Although existential philosophy and psychoanalysis are often thought of as incompatible fields, Thompson shows how they share far more in common than is usually supposed. This volume will help clinicians, scholars, and students of all persuasions learn how integrating the two disciplines introduces a more personal and revolutionary understanding of what psychoanalysis can be in the twenty-first century.

This compelling assimilation of continental philosophy and psychoanalysis will be of interest to psychoanalytic practitioners and psychotherapists, as well as philosophers, social scientists and any student of the human condition.

M. Guy Thompson is the founder and Director of the New School for Existential Psychoanalysis, and a Personal and Supervising Analyst and Faculty Member at the Psychoanalytic Institute of Northern California, San Francisco, USA. He is the author of *Essays in Existential Psychoanalysis: On the Primacy of Authenticity* (2023) and *The Death of Desire: An Existential Study in Sanity and Madness* (second edition, 2016), and the editor of *The Legacy of R. D. Laing: An Appraisal of His Contemporary Relevance* (2015).

Routledge Introductions to Contemporary Psychoanalysis

Series Editor: Aner Govrin
Executive Editor: Yael Peri Herzovich

This comprehensive series illuminates the intricate landscape of psychoanalytic theory and practice. In this collection of concise yet illuminating volumes, we delve into the influential figures, groundbreaking concepts, and transformative theories that shape the contemporary psychoanalytic landscape. At the heart of each volume lies a commitment to clarity, accessibility, and depth. Our expert authors, renowned scholars and practitioners in their respective fields, guide readers through the complexities of psychoanalytic thought with precision and enthusiasm. Whether you are a seasoned psychoanalyst, a student eager to explore the field, or a curious reader seeking insight into the human psyche, our series offers a wealth of knowledge and insight.

Schizophrenia
A Contemporary Introduction
Gillian Steggles

Erotic Transferences
A Contemporary Introduction
Andrea Celenza

Otto Kernberg
A Contemporary Introduction
Frank Yeomans, Diana Diamond and Eve Caligor

Erich Fromm
A Contemporary Introduction
Sandra Buechler

Narcissism
A Contemporary Introduction
Richard Wood

The Death Drive
A Contemporary Introduction
Rossella Valdrè

Depression
A Contemporary Introduction
Marianne Leuzinger-Bohleber

Ronald Fairbairn
A Contemporary Introduction
David P. Celani

The Evidence for Psychodynamic Psychotherapy
A Contemporary Introduction
Kevin McCarthy, Carla Capone and Liat Liebovich

Psychoanalytic Group Psychotherapy
A Contemporary Introduction
Richard M. Billow

Existential Psychoanalysis
A Contemporary Introduction
M. Guy Thompson

For more information about this series, please visit: https://www.routledge.com/Routledge-Introductions-to-Contemporary-Psychoanalysis/book-series/ICP

Existential Psychoanalysis

A Contemporary Introduction

M. Guy Thompson

Routledge
Taylor & Francis Group
LONDON AND NEW YORK

Designed cover image: © Michal Heiman, Asylum 1855–2020, The Sleeper (video, psychoanalytic sofa and Plate 34), exhibition view, Herzliya Museum of Contemporary Art, 2017

First published 2025
by Routledge
4 Park Square, Milton Park, Abingdon, Oxon OX14 4RN

and by Routledge
605 Third Avenue, New York, NY 10158

Routledge is an imprint of the Taylor & Francis Group, an informa business

© 2025 M. Guy Thompson

All rights reserved. No part of this book may be reprinted or reproduced or utilised in any form or by any electronic, mechanical, or other means, now known or hereafter invented, including photocopying and recording, or in any information storage or retrieval system, without permission in writing from the publishers.

Trademark notice: Product or corporate names may be trademarks or registered trademarks, and are used only for identification and explanation without intent to infringe.

British Library Cataloguing-in-Publication Data
A catalogue record for this book is available from the British Library

ISBN: 978-1-032-97784-3 (hbk)
ISBN: 978-1-032-97786-7 (pbk)
ISBN: 978-1-003-59542-7 (ebk)

DOI: 10.4324/9781003595427

Typeset in Times New Roman
by Taylor & Francis Books

Contents

	Series Editor's Preface	x
	ANER GOVRIN	
	Preface	xii
	Acknowledgements	xvii
1	What Is Existential Psychoanalysis?	1
2	Sartre and Psychoanalysis	26
3	Vicissitudes of Authenticity	43
4	The Demise of the Person in Psychoanalysis	81
	Conclusion	106
	Index	110

Series Editor's Preface

Aner Govrin

Routledge Introductions to Contemporary Psychoanalysis is one of the most prominent psychoanalytic publishing ventures of our day. The series' aim is to become an encyclopedia of psychoanalysis, with each entry given its own book.

Each volume serves as a gateway into a specific aspect of psychoanalytic theory and practice. From the pioneering works of Sigmund Freud to the innovative contributions of modern theorists such as Antonino Ferro and Michal Eigen, our series covers a diverse range of topics, including seminal figures, key concepts, and emerging trends. Whether you are interested in classical psychoanalysis, object relations theory, or the intersection of neuroscience and psychoanalysis, you will find a wealth of resources within our collection.

One of the hallmarks of our series is its interdisciplinary approach. While rooted in psychoanalytic theory, our volumes draw upon insights from psychology, philosophy, sociology, and other disciplines to offer a holistic understanding of the human mind and its complexities.

Each volume in the series is crafted with the reader in mind, balancing scholarly rigor with engaging prose. Whether you are embarking on your journey into psychoanalysis or seeking to deepen your understanding of specific topics, our series provides a clear and comprehensive roadmap.

Moreover, our series is committed to fostering dialogue and debate within the psychoanalytic community. Each volume invites readers to critically engage with the material, encouraging reflection, discussion, and further exploration.

We invite you to join us on this journey of discovery as we explore the ever-evolving landscape of psychoanalysis.

Preface

Existential psychoanalysis is an integration of existential philosophy and psychoanalysis. There is no existing critique about which I am aware that integrates the two disciplines until now, with the book you hold in your hands. In the post-World War II era a handful of German and French psychiatrists, led by Ludwig Binswanger and Medard Boss, who were both psychoanalytically trained, attempted to formulate an integration of Freud and Heidegger.[1] However, their work sought simply to "correct" Freud's metapsychology by dismissing his conceptions of the *unconscious* and *transference* phenomena, cardinal principals of psychoanalysis. Rather than a concerted *integration* of Heidegger and Freud, they attempted to reframe Freud's concepts by virtually doing away with them. In order to be successful, a proper integration of existential philosophy and psychoanalysis must necessarily embody a broader treatment of existential philosophy than relying on Heidegger alone. (As you will see in this *Introduction to Existential Psychoanalysis*, I make liberal use of Friedrich Nietzsche and Jean-Paul Sartre throughout this volume, as well as Martin Heidegger.) Moreover, the concepts of transference phenomena and the unconscious must be retained, but reformulated, not eradicated altogether. Without a conception of the unconscious and the transference, one cannot formulate an existential *psychoanalysis*.

This is no doubt why neither Binswanger nor Boss — Swiss psychiatrists who were close to both Freud and Jung — labeled their clinical theories an "existential psychoanalysis." Binswanger adopted the label *existential analysis*, whereas Boss adopted *daseinsanalysis*, an obvious nod to Heidegger's notion of Dasein, a uniquely Heideggerian conception of selfhood. It appears that no one believed the two disciplines, existential philosophy and psychoanalysis, could be integrated. That is, until R. D. Laing came along.

Laing was a Scottish psychoanalyst who became famous in the late 1960s and 1970s with the publication of *The Divided Self* (1960 [1969]), *Self and Others* (1961 [1969]), *Sanity, Madness and the Family* (1964 [1970] with Aaron Esterson), and *The Politics of Experience* (1967), among other works, all published in the 1960s. Being passionate about both existential philosophy and Sigmund Freud since adolescence, I had hoped from an early age to fashion an integration between the two. However, while a graduate student studying clinical psychology in the early 1970s in San Francisco, I discovered the work of R. D. Laing when I came across a copy of *The Divided Self*. Upon reading this book I realized that Laing had already integrated existential philosophy and psychoanalysis. I subsequently abandoned my graduate studies and moved to London in order to work with him, and to undergo my training in existential psychoanalysis with Laing and his cohorts at the Philadelphia Association.

Yet Laing was hesitant to actually call himself an existential psychoanalyst, preferring to simply refer to himself as a psychoanalyst. This was because by the 1970s Laing believed the term "existential" had become too broad to enjoy a discernable definition. He opted instead to employ the term "phenomenology" as a replacement for "existential."[2] I see the logic in this decision, and perhaps half a century ago this made sense, when a plethora of existential "therapy" training programs emerged in the UK, ironically due to Laing's influence. All of these programs were hostile to psychoanalysis. But we are now in 2024, and the term "existential" — at least to American ears — today enjoys a certain resonance and mystique. No one is quite sure what it means, so I set out to address this in my first chapter, "What Is Existential Psychoanalysis?"

The fact is, there is no underlying theory of existential psychoanalysis, nor is there a discernable technique. All psychoanalytic schools, including Freudian, Kleinian, Winnicottian, Bionian, Lacanian, Kohutian, and so on, are distinguished from the others by identifiable theories and techniques. The integration of existential philosophy and psychoanalysis enjoys no *universal* theory and technique. Existential psychoanalysis has no technique. This is what makes it *existential*. It is far too personal, intimate, and informal to "apply" techniques to one's clinical practice with other human beings. The use of the couch, the frequency of sessions, the restricted nature of the dialogue between analyst and patient all go out the window. It is up to each practitioner to determine how he or she seeks to fashion the relationship between them. Similarly, theory necessarily plays a role in any analyst's education and published work, as it does mine. But such theoretical considerations will necessarily vary from existential psychoanalyst to existential psychoanalyst. I describe the way that *I* integrate the two throughout this work.

Despite all the bad press that he still suffers, I feel indebted to Sigmund Freud, and I consider Freud a visionary who was far ahead of his time, and still is, yet sorely misunderstood. I don't have a problem with his terminology, but I found that in order to really grasp what Freud was on about one really needs to read his entire work, from start to finish, with a sympathetic ear. Despite all the rhetoric about his reduction of the human condition to a biological conception of sexuality, I discovered that what Freud was really wrestling with throughout his lifetime was the relationship between love and psychopathology: human suffering. Freud is the only psychoanalyst who insisted that virtually all forms of mental and emotional distress derive from unrequited love: a broken heart. After more than fifty years of clinical work, I have to say that I more or less agree with Freud. Love, and its absence, determines virtually every aspect of our lives. But talking about it isn't so easy. The word "love" is just too loaded with connotations, ambiguities, and associations to employ in a scientific fashion, so you rarely see that word mentioned in conventional psychoanalytic publications. Not all psychoanalysts even agree that love is a good thing!

Why do people seek therapy in the first place? Generally, when someone suffers a personal crisis in a relationship or a job, or is chronically anxious or depressed, or simply unhappy or miserable with his or her life, that person often seeks someone to talk to. For most people, taking someone into their confidence — as they would a friend — offers some comfort, and over time new ways of seeing things. Once their crisis mitigates they often stop therapy, getting what they came for. But others may be more ambitious, or desperate, or reflective. And they may have come to conclude that their problems are deeper and more chronic than they had realized before therapy. Brief, problem-solving therapies are of little use to them. For them, they require a deeper kind of therapy, psychoanalysis, in order to get to the bottom of their suffering and eventually access a deeper confidence in themselves. They seek to feel more alive, less risk-averse, less judgmental, more loving. This takes time. And it also requires finding a psychoanalyst they can trust, with whom they feel a profound connection. In my view, there is no better type of psychotherapy that achieves this goal than *existential psychoanalysis*.

You will note in the following chapters that I do not offer clinical vignettes to demonstrate how I work, with verbatim process notes that serve to give examples of what sets an existential psychoanalyst apart from other psychoanalysts or existential therapists. Because I do not adopt a technique, I have no techniques to demonstrate. I will explain why this is so in Chapter Four of this book, where I explore what I take to be a *person*, and the inherently personal dimension to existential psychoanalysis.

In Chapter One, "What Is Existential Psychoanalysis?" I set out to define how I employ the term "existential" in this book, and moreover to distinguish the differences, as I understand them, between *psycho*analysis and *existential* psychoanalysis. I also set out to distinguish the differences between existential *psychoanalysis* and non-psychodynamic *therapies*. However, it will require reading this entire book in order to grasp these distinctions, as I employ them.

In Chapter Two, "Sartre and Psychoanalysis," I review the important role that Jean-Paul Sartre, the existential philosopher, plays in conceptualizing what an existential approach to psychoanalysis properly entails.

In Chapter Three, "Vicissitudes of Authenticity," I review the core concept of what sets existential psychoanalysis apart from other schools of psychoanalysis. But I also seek to show the role that authenticity surreptitiously plays in the psychoanalytic theories of psychoanalysts who are not explicitly identified with existentialism, such as Sigmund Freud, D. W. Winnicott, Wilfried Bion, and Jacques Lacan.

And Finally, in Chapter Four, "The Demise of the Person in Psychoanalysis," I set out to show how the prevailing psychoanalytic conceptions of the unconscious and transference phenomena have served to delete the very notion of a personal dimension to the relationship between analyst and patient, and how an existential conception of psychoanalysis corrects this problem.

With this brief Preface, I leave you, my reader, to enjoy this book, the very first introduction to *existential psychoanalysis* ever undertaken, as far as I know. Please read it from start to finish before forming an opinion. I think you will be rewarded for doing so.

Notes

1 See Binswanger, L. (1963) *Being-in-the-world: Selected papers of Ludwig Binswanger* (J. Needleman, trans.). New York: Basic Books; Boss, M. (1963) *Psychoanalysis and daseinsanalysis* (L. Lefebre, trans.). New York: Basic Books.
2 I treat the relation between existential philosophy and phenomenology at length in the first chapter of this book.

References

Binswanger, L. (1963) *Being-in-the-world: Selected papers of Ludwig Binswanger* (J. Needleman, trans.). New York: Basic Books.

Boss, M. (1963) *Psychoanalysis and daseinsanalysis* (L. Lefebre, trans.). New York: Basic Books.

Laing, R. D. (1960 [1969]) *The divided self.* New York and London: Penguin Books.

Laing, R. D. (1961 [1969]) *Self and others.* New York and London: Penguin Books.

Laing, R. D. (1967) *The politics of experience.* New York: Pantheon Books.

Laing, R. D. and Esterson, A. (1964 [1970]) *Sanity, madness and the family.* New York and London: Penguin Books.

Acknowledgements

An earlier version of Chapter Three was previously published in *Contemporary Psychoanalysis* as "Vicissitudes of Authenticity in the Psychoanalytic Situation," Volume *42*, No. *2*: 139–176, 2006.

I want to especially thank my editor at Routledge, Aner Govrin, for his advocacy of this project, and his guidance.

Chapter 1

What Is Existential Psychoanalysis?

What do we mean when we employ the term *existential*? What relevance does it have for clinical practice? By invoking it, what are we are trying to convey about the way we conceive the therapeutic process? Psychoanalysis had someone, Sigmund Freud, to invent it. But no one is credited with inventing existentialism, as a philosophical school or as simply a concept. Yet existential philosophy is the foundation for the various therapies that are identified with it, including existential therapy, existential analysis, daseinsanalysis, existential psychoanalysis, and so on. I'll admit that I'm not too crazy about any of these designations. Just as there is no one philosopher who can be credited with having invented existentialism, there is no one who can be credited with having invented existential therapy. This makes it highly problematic to define just what performing therapy from an existential perspective should look like, because there is no general agreement as to what existential philosophy is, nor what existential therapy should be.

As psychoanalysis was created by Freud, for a great deal of his lifetime he was able to dictate what it was and what it was not. A number of Freud's followers, including C. G. Jung, Alfred Adler, and Otto Rank, broke with Freud when they began to develop ideas that were contrary to his, especially Freud's emphasis on sexuality as the *sine qua non* of the human condition. Because Freud got to define what psychoanalysis was, anyone who disagreed with him could be accused of no longer adhering to psychoanalytic principles as delineated by him.

DOI: 10.4324/9781003595427-1

Since Freud's death, however, this is no longer the case. There is wide latitude today as to what psychoanalysis is and who may call themselves a psychoanalyst. Yet, because Freud invented it and provided all of its fundamental concepts, including the unconscious and the transference, analysts today are obliged to situate their perspective within the context of Freud's, to articulate those areas with which they are in agreement and those where they are not. Even if what we call psychoanalysis today enjoys enormous elasticity (so long as the unconscious and the transference are accounted for), Freud's writings nonetheless serve to provide the foundational texts from which all subsequent theories are derived, even if no one nowadays bothers to read Freud first hand. This provides the psychoanalytic perspective, whatever it is and however defined by this or that practitioner, with a sense of integrity. The same cannot be said for therapies that are identified with existentialism. Existential therapy, or therapy practiced from an existential sensibility, can be more or less whatever anyone claims it is, which may account for why, as a therapeutic movement, it has not been nearly as popular or influential as psychoanalysis has been.

Existentialism became fashionable in the post-World War II era, first in Europe, then gradually across the Atlantic to the Americas. As an adjective for *existence*, the word existential became a technical term that was descriptive of a philosophical school popularized by Jean-Paul Sartre with the publication of his magnum opus, *Being and Nothingness*, first published in France in 1943, two years before the end of the war. Though Sartre was the first philosopher to call himself an existentialist, he did not invent the label. The term was first coined by the French Catholic philosopher Gabriel Marcel in the mid-1940s, but it was Sartre with whom existentialism is most identified. *L'existentialisme* became all the rage in Paris and served to epitomize the hip, *Bohemian*, Parisian café-set of intellectuals, *artistes*, and vagabonds who ushered in an age of non-conformity, a kind of societal and intellectual rebellion against chains, first imposed by the Germans during the Nazi occupation of France, then by any form of orthodoxy that presumed to dictate what people should believe and how they were to behave. Paris became a philosophical culture and *l'existentialisme* dripped from the lips of anyone who presumed to be in-the-know and a member of the chic, *avant-garde* set of Parisian society to which everyone who was anyone wanted to belong. Sartre held center stage of this tribe of intellectuals at his favorite café, *Café de Flore*, where he sipped espresso while crafting his most famous philosophical and literary works.

Sartre — along with his close friend, Maurice Merleau-Ponty, and lover, Simone de Beauvoir — may have made existentialism famous, but it anticipated them by more than a century. Though it is difficult to claim that any one person invented existentialism, it would be hard to contest that there were four principal philosophers who generated what came to be known as existential philosophy, each with his own singular contribution. The Danish nineteenth-century philosopher, Soren Kierkegaard, is generally credited as the first philosopher to articulate a philosophy that contained all the elements that we associate with this perspective, including his emphasis on freedom, agency, and authenticity. He did not, however, coin the label "existentialism" nor use it to depict his take on the human condition. Kierkegaard was followed by another nineteenth-century philosopher, the German Friedrich Nietzsche. It isn't clear whether Nietzsche ever read any of Kierkegaard's works, though he was aware of Kierkegaard and spoke of him. Both philosophers were opposed to the abstraction of traditional philosophy, epitomized by a German philosopher whom they detested, Georg Wilhelm Friedrich Hegel, and sought instead to emphasize the inherently personal aspects of philosophy and the importance of facing anxiety authentically, which is to say, honestly. The twentieth-century philosopher Martin Heidegger was probably the most important thinker in the existential tradition due to the volume of his output, the radical nature of his ideas, and his emphasis on the role of existence in everyday human affairs. Unlike Kierkegaard and Nietzsche, Heidegger deliberately employed the term "existential" in his work and assigned it a specific philosophical meaning. Moreover, Heidegger was thoroughly steeped in both Kierkegaard's and Nietzsche's writings and made liberal use of both of them. Kierkegaard's views about anxiety, authenticity, and the nature of the self profoundly influenced Heidegger's thinking and Heidegger's reading of Nietzsche in turn had considerable impact on contemporary perceptions of Nietzsche's philosophy. Sartre's main philosophical work, *Being and Nothingness* (1943 [1954]), is almost a verbatim French version of Division II of Heidegger's magnum opus, *Being and Time* (1927 [1962]), which deals with concepts such as freedom and authenticity, though Sartre was also significantly influenced by Heidegger's teacher, Edmund Husserl (more about him later). It was Sartre who popularized existential philosophy and turned it into a cultural phenomenon which, in turn, brought Kierkegaard, Nietzsche, and Heidegger to the non-academic public's attention for the first time.

Another philosopher who is important in the development of existentialism is the German, Karl Jaspers, a contemporary of Heidegger's and close friend of another woman who is closely associated with existentialism, Hannah Arendt, a student of Heidegger's with whom he had an affair. Jaspers was overshadowed by Heidegger's unprecedented celebrity so is better known as a psychiatrist who wrote a seminal work on psychopathology. There are many more philosophers as well as literary authors who are associated with existentialism, including Spain's Miguel de Unamuno and Jose Ortega y Gasset, the Bohemian, Franz Kafka, a novelist who was famous for his masterpiece, *The Trial*, and Albert Camus, another French thinker and novelist, famous for *The Stranger*. Others include Martin Buber, the philosopher and Jewish theologian, Paul Tillich, another philosopher and theologian, but a Christian, the Russian Fyodor Dostoyevsky, considered by some the first existentialist, Franz Fanon, Immanuel Levinas, and others too many to mention. This of course does not exhaust all the other names, non-philosophical novelists and artists who can be included as having embodied what I am calling an *existentialist sensibility*, including the American writers Ernest Hemingway, Dashiell Hammett, Jim Thompson, Philip K. Dick, the painters Pablo Picasso, Salvador Dali, Paul Cezanne, Francis Bacon, William Blake, Jackson Pollock, Andy Warhol, the poets Samuel Beckett and Richard Wright, filmmakers such as Ingmar Bergman, Luis Bunuel, Federico Fellini, Francois Truffaut, Alain Resnais, Alfred Hitchcock, Stanley Kubrick, and, of course, Woody Allen. We could spend all day compiling a list of twentieth-century artists, thinkers, and authors who embody an existential perspective, but I will spare you that. The second half of the twentieth century is dominated by this sensibility, due to the two world wars that preceded it, the Cold War that dominated the second half of the century, and the industrial revolution that preceded both. It was difficult to be a thoughtful person in the twentieth century and not be preoccupied with existential concerns: life, death, and the meaning of it all.

So what *is* existentialism? What can we say about the existential perspective, or sensibility, despite so many philosophers who are associated with it? Because there is no orthodox encapsulation of what it means, I can only tell you what it means to me. Every philosophical perspective has its nomenclature, terms that set it apart from others, though there is often overlap. This is no less true for existentialism. The words I most readily associate with this perspective, though not exhaustive, are the following.

I will begin with the word *experience*. Experience is privileged in existential thinkers because it is inherently personal and not as abstract and academic as other philosophies, which is what sets it apart from other philosophical schools. Though this sometimes makes existential philosophy more accessible to the layman, Heidegger's *Being and Time* is considered the most difficult philosophical work ever written to understand. Whatever else the existential perspective embodies, it is primarily concerned with *my* way of seeing things, which is the only way of seeing things that I have direct access to. The concept of experience was a favorite of R. D. Laing's and so important to him that it was included in the title of two of his books, *The Politics of Experience* (1967 [1983]) and *The Voice of Experience* (1982).

Experience is closely associated with another term you see frequently employed by existentialists, but by no means exclusively: the word *meaning*. Things matter to me, which is another way of saying the world I live in *means* something to *me*. What it means is up to me to determine, and only I can do so. The search for meaning, specifically what my life is about, is probably the most basic topic explored in both existential therapies as well as psychoanalysis, each of which sees the therapeutic process as one of getting to know oneself in the most fundamental way possible.

Another is the term, *authenticity*. All existentialist thinkers promote authenticity over inauthenticity, but there is little agreement as to what authenticity is. First and foremost it is a way of articulating what it means to be honest with oneself. Honesty was highly valued by Freud, and one could argue that he promoted authenticity in his patients' lives via the act of free association, disclosing whatever is on one's mind to another person. Both psychoanalysis and existentialism are concerned with becoming the person you are, by dropping the pretenses we typically employ to please others. This is probably the feature of both these disciplines that has made them so controversial. Each acts as a subversive element in society by helping the members of that society separate themselves from the status quo. No group enjoys group members pissing on what that group is about, which is why groups are conservative in nature. Perhaps this explains why existentialists tend to be fiercely independent and avoid groups as a rule.

Authenticity is also closely linked to the existential preoccupation with the concept of *freedom*. This is a complicated and generally misunderstood concept. Like authenticity, various existential thinkers differ in how they see it. For the most part, to be free in the existential sense is to realize that I *choose* to be who I am at the deepest, most fundamental level of my being, though I usually deny this, a common ploy in psychotherapy. This doesn't mean I am always *conscious* of my choices, as they typically operate under the surface of awareness. This implies that I have *agency* in my actions, that I am behind my acts, impressions, and attitudes about the life I live and therefore I am responsible for who I am and what I do. I even choose my neuroses! A man in prison may feel trapped and unable to escape, but he nonetheless chooses how he reacts to being a prisoner, whether to become embittered or to improve himself, or to try and escape against all odds.

Another term that is closely associated with the existential perspective is the German word, *Angst*. We typically translate this as anxiety in English, but it can also mean anguish. Human beings are inherently anxious and this is a fundamental aspect of our being. This is similar to Freud's contention that all of us are anxious creatures who relentlessly seek to minimize that anxiety as much as we can, often to our detriment. Though the terminology adopted by existential philosophy and psychoanalysis differ, their respective ways of privileging anxiety as an ongoing problem with which all of us grapple is complementary. For the most part they both agree that anxiety is a good thing and that we need to learn how to attend to and accommodate it rather than eliminating or minimizing it. Naturally, when we *suffer* anxiety we instinctively want to suppress it, but existentialism and psychoanalysis, like Buddhism, embrace suffering as a vital constituent of life that begs to be understood, without sedatives.

The last word I associate with existentialism is *alienation*, yet another term that is not used exclusively by existentialists. Humans are inherently *estranged* from, while being fundamentally *rooted in* their environment. Alienation is also a key theme in Marxism, but for different reasons. Marx argued that our alienation in society is due to the inequity of social classes and economic privilege. Existentialists locate our alienation in the encroaching power of technology that threatens to turn people into machines. Though this problem originated in the industrial revolution, it is also a popular theme among science fiction writers, such as Phillip K. Dick, who explored how the distinction between humans and machines may disappear in the not too distant future, in a world where, says Dick, "machines are more human than humans."[1] On a more basic level, we are alienated from each other because we can never really know each other, nor ourselves. We are inherent strangers to each other and mistake who we take each other to be through the projections we confer on one another. Whether this is fixable or not varies among existential thinkers, some arguing there is no escape, others suggesting we are capable of bridging our estrangement from one another though love. The most basic problem, however, is our estrangement from ourselves, because we do not really know ourselves any better than we know others, perhaps even less. This alludes to the problem of authenticity and how the inauthentic individual is estranged from himself, but needn't be, as long as he or she chooses to do something about it.

What all of these terms share in common is that they are perfectly ordinary terms that we use all the time. This is what made existentialism so popular in its heyday. Each of us grapples with these concerns throughout our lives. Any thinking person who has not encountered existential literature is nonetheless, as it were, a closet existentialist, she just doesn't know it. It would be difficult to be a thoughtful human being and not be. Despite the variety of thinkers who are associated with an existential perspective and their diversity, what is the common outlook about life that links them together? In the main, all of these thinkers would agree that life challenges us from the moment we are born with pain, frustration, and disappointment, and that it confronts us with tasks that are extremely difficult to perform, and which leave scars that are impossible to erase. Though as children we are convinced things will become easier as we grow older, experience teaches us the opposite, that life becomes increasingly more difficult, and that this state of affairs persists throughout our existence until finally we are faced with the inevitability of our death. Whether you are religious or an atheist makes no difference in the existentialist's attitude about death. For the atheist, like Sartre, life has no intrinsic meaning and all we can say is that life is what we make of it, then we die. For a Christian existentialist such as Kierkegaard, Gabriel Marcel, or Paul Tillich, believing in God may provide a measure of comfort, but religious belief being rooted in faith rather than fact (it is a fact, for example, that I am going to die, but not that God exists) means that, because I am human, I cannot escape those moments of doubt that San Juan de la Cruz depicted so well in *The Dark Night of the Soul* (2003). This is the despair I feel when I sense that I may very well be alone in the universe because God, if there is one, doesn't speak to me, or if he once did, has now abandoned me. Nietzsche's famous pronouncement that "God is dead" was his way of letting us know it is about time we take responsibility for our lives and stop leaning on external authorities to tell us what to do, or to save us. Despite Nietzsche's opinion on the matter, the existential position is that it is possible, perhaps inevitable, to do that whether or not one believes in God.

If there is one theme that pervades just about every existentialist thinker or artist, it is that we are unremittingly alone in this world, whatever I believe awaits me after I die, and this sense of aloneness is something I cannot nor should I deny. It is where I live in the deepest recesses of my self-identity. The ways that I cope with this aloneness makes me the person I am and says more about me and who I am than the most detailed biography ever could. This is the basis of the despair that Kierkegaard described so effectively in *The Sickness Unto Death* (1980) and that every existentialist philosopher has identified with since. Is there a cure for this despair? Because despair is not a clinical diagnosis but a fundamental aspect of my nature it is something that will always be a part of me. Some may react to it with an increase of anxiety or depression, give up and turn to drugs or other distractions to cope with the pain of it. Others may turn to philosophy, religion, or artistic endeavors to turn their despair into something meaningful that can paradoxically enrich their life and make it more valuable and rewarding. Others still may turn to psychoanalysis or other kinds of therapy, including existential, believing there is something the matter with them for feeling this way. Or they may recognize they are struggling with anxieties inherent in living and simply want someone they can talk to about it. However, in order to turn to anyone for help when burdened with such despair, they must first be *aware* of it. Most people, says Nietzsche, go through life as though in a dream, oblivious of the incredible pain they are in. Such a person needs to wake up. But no one can do that for him. One can only wake up oneself.

It has been argued that existentialism and, for that matter, phenomenology have their origins in Greek thought, going back to Socrates. Edmund Husserl, the father of phenomenology and former teacher of Heidegger's, borrowed his method of bracketing, the *epoché*, from the Greek skeptics. The skeptics came after Socrates,[2] and we can trace their origins to the way Socrates liked to engage the philosophers of his day in conversation, asking them how they knew the things they professed to. No matter how astute his opponents were, Socrates always succeeded in humiliating them by showing they relied solely on theory and speculation, but not incontrovertible truths. Socrates professed to know nothing, except that he was smart enough to recognize how ignorant he was, which was more than he could say about the philosophers he typically encountered, who were called Sophists. Because this method of conversing aimed to pare away false assumptions, this method planted the seeds for what would subsequently become the skeptic method of inquiry, the *epoché*, initiated by Pyrrho about a century after Socrates.

But Socrates was also the first existentialist in the manner he sought to separate philosophy from religion, by looking for secular explanations about the meaning of life. In Plato's dialogues Socrates ranges over all manner of topics, including the meaning of happiness, love, courage, integrity, morality, and so on, none of which rely on religious explanations as to what life is about. This was a radical and apparently dangerous position to take because everything that occurred in Greek culture was explained by the gods and goddesses on Olympus. Before Socrates the Greeks believed that every human endeavor was supposed to have its origin in one's relationship with Greek deities. Though Socrates paid lip-service to their existence, what distinguished philosophy from religion was its alternative, inherently secular world view. Despite his efforts to placate his less sophisticated Athenian citizens, Socrates was eventually brought up on charges in his old age for allegedly corrupting the youth and preaching false religions (an allusion to Socrates' invention of mythological characters with which to buttress some of his arguments). Socrates could have avoided execution by apologizing for his misdeeds, but being a man of integrity he refused to do this and insisted he was doing his fellow Athenians a favor by educating their youth! This only inflamed his accusers further and, as he gave them no way out, Socrates was reluctantly executed. In death Socrates became a martyr and epitomized the way subsequent philosophers sought to defend the truth as they saw it. Other philosophers in the centuries that followed were executed for similar transgressions. It is not coincidental that existentialists such as Nietzsche and Heidegger turn to the Greeks as the source of their own world view, including the skeptic sensibility that Socrates epitomized.

We are now ready to look at those clinicians identified with the existential tradition, as well as some who are not but nevertheless demonstrate an existential sensibility. First I should clarify how I employ the term "existential" in this book. I do not make a direct correlation between this term and any one of the existential philosophers listed above, though I draw from many of them, including Heidegger, Sartre, Nietzsche, Kierkegaard, Scheler, Merleau-Ponty, and others. For the purposes of this book and the chapters that comprise it, I use the term broadly, sometimes figuratively. For example, there are a number of psychoanalysts whom I believe embody what I call an existential *sensibility*, in certain if not all aspects of their clinical work. Apart from Laing and those analysts who explicitly identify themselves with the existential philosophical tradition, I include D. W. Winnicott, Wilfried Bion, Jacques Lacan, Hans Loewald, Stanley Leavy, Martin Bergmann, Harry Stack Sullivan, Otto Allen Will, Jr., Edgar Levenson, Eric Fromm, Frieda Fromm-Reichmann, Clara Thompson, even Sigmund Freud as only some of the analysts who embody an existential perspective in their approach to clinical practice. I could go over each one of them and identify those aspects of their thinking that I identify as existential, but I don't think I need to bother with that because it should be abundantly clear how I would do this by the time you have finished reading this book. I want to use the remainder of this chapter to highlight some of the general features of what I mean by an existential sensibility and how that is employed in this volume.

My thesis is that the terms personal and existential, for the purposes of this study, should be treated synonymously. Both psychoanalytic and non-psychoanalytic schools of therapy are riddled with techniques. I am not saying they do not have their place. I consider Freud's technical recommendations, especially free association, neutrality, abstinence, and transference, to be compatible with an existential way of conducting therapy. But even these technical principles have been sorely misunderstood by psychoanalysts by reading into them strict guidelines on how analysts are expected to behave if they expect to be conducting a *psychoanalysis*. In fact, Freud stated quite clearly that his technical recommendations should be molded to the personality of each analyst. He did not say that the analyst's personality should be molded to his technical recommendations. Yet, that is precisely how analysts typically behave. Virtually all of the schools of psychotherapy that have evolved since Freud inaugurated this profession have followed suit, whether behavioral or cognitive, and even many of the other contemporary non-psychoanalytic schools of existential therapy.

In my view, existential psychoanalysis is essentially *conversational*, not technical. Conversing is not a technique. It is spontaneous, relaxed, curious, non-judgmental, and open-minded. These are not rules. This is the way we ordinarily talk to others. It is the most intimate activity that any two human beings can conduct with each other. The word intimate is both a noun and a verb. Our relationship may be intimate, and I may also *intimate* to you something that I want to say. To intimate is to converse, to engage in conversation. This is why confession is so essential to Catholicism, when one human being is baring his or her soul to another human being. It is the heart and soul of psychoanalysis, the talking cure. This is also why I regard Freud as perhaps the very first existential psychoanalyst. He got this. For the most part, his followers did not.

This is why the person of each existential psychoanalyst is not only important. It is essential. We work from the heart, not a book of rules. Much of the curative power of this form of therapy is epitomized by the heart to heart connection fashioned between therapist and patient. It is up to the therapist to try his or her best to make this happen. Each of us brings unique gifts into this equation, because each of us is unique. You might say that our entire childhood was a kind of training to eventually become an existential psychoanalyst. Let me take a moment to share how this applies to me.

As I have said, my approach to clinical practice is a hybrid of psychoanalysis and the existential philosophical tradition. This is an odd combination, to say the least, and I may be among the few people in the world who see psychoanalysis as deriving from that tradition.[3] I first encountered Freud when I was sixteen and looking for something to read about sex, a topic that was then in the forefront of my attention. I discovered that he had written a book titled *Three Essays on the Theory of Sexuality* (1905 [1953]). It wasn't exactly what I was looking for, but the book held me spellbound and completely changed the way I understood sex. It so happened that while I was reading my first book by Freud I had also stumbled upon a book by Sartre titled *Nausea* (1964). All I knew about Sartre at the time was that he was associated with existentialism. I hadn't a clue what existentialism was but I was drawn to the word and wanted to know more about it. Because it whetted my appetite for more I found another book by Sartre, titled *Sketch for a Theory of the Emotions* (1962). Somehow, as I was reading these three books simultaneously, I came away with a sense that both Sartre and Freud, existentialist and psychoanalyst, were talking about the same thing, though employing different terminology. They were talking about a lot of the things I was feeling at the time and struggling with: anxiety, frustration, desire, disappointment, boredom. I decided then and there that I wanted to be a philosopher and that somehow or other this would be my vocation, once I became an adult.

Unfortunately, I was stuck in a small town in Tennessee and the only access I had to ideas was the local library which, you might imagine, was lacking in philosophical or psychoanalytic works. Tennessee was foreign to me and I was not a happy camper. My family had moved to Havana, Cuba when I was a year old due to a business venture that took my father to that faraway island. He was a chemical engineer and went to Cuba from New York, where we lived at the time, to build a textile plant. A year later, by the time the project was completed, my father had fallen in love with Cuban culture and decided to live there, so that is where I spent my childhood until just before my fourteenth birthday, when we returned to, you guessed it, Tennessee, where my parents were from. The culture shock from Cuba to Tennessee was devastating for a fledgling teenager. Cuba was amazing and a magical place for a child to grow up. Cubans were sexy, stylish, playful, intelligent, classy. Havana was breathtakingly beautiful and a playground for the rich or adventurous. As they were among the few ex-patriot Americans on the island, my parents became friends with Ernest Hemingway and his wife, Mary, and my father brought me along with him occasionally when he met Hemingway at the Floridita Bar in Old Havana for daiquiris. I adored Hemingway and loved to hear his stories about living in Paris and Spain, places I longed to visit. I didn't quite register this at the time, but he also spoke of a French philosopher and novelist who was a friend of his and happened to be visiting Cuba with his girlfriend, Simon de Beauvoir. It was only later, when I found Sartre's book in the Elizabethton, Tennessee library that I realized this was the thinker Hemingway had been talking about.

Trying to adjust to a tiny little town in East Tennessee after the exotic and sophisticated Havana threw me into an existential crisis. Who was I and what was I doing there? I felt *Angst*, boredom, dislocation. A year after we returned to Tennessee from

Cuba, two years before my encounter with Freud and Sartre, my mother, who struggled with depression all her life, killed herself. I was fourteen. My mother was everything to me and the loss was catastrophic. I cannot remember the first time my mother told me she wanted to kill herself, and relented when I pleaded with her not to. Now and then she would take an overdose of pills anyway, but recovered, only to try again at some unpredictable time. It was as though my childhood was devoted to keeping my mother alive, until that fateful day in Tennessee when she shot herself and died six days later. In effect, my mother was training me to be her therapist, to give her hope.

After leaving Cuba my mother and my father divorced, and I remained with her in Tennessee when my father returned to New York. I initially blamed my father for her death, so instead of opting to live with him I stayed in Tennessee and lived with my maternal grandparents, with whom I had always been close. It was during this hiatus, wondering what life had in store for me next, that I began looking for answers in this small town library. It was around this time that John F. Kennedy discovered the Soviet Union had planted missiles in Cuba, initiating the Cuban Missile Crisis. Everyone was convinced we were about to enter a nuclear war with Russia and that once it commenced every eligible American male from fifteen to fifty would be drafted into service. The crisis passed, but soon after Kennedy was assassinated and the world came apart all over again.

I'm just trying to paint you a picture, a portrait of what my life was like at the time I discovered existentialism and psychoanalysis, the two disciplines that were to dominate my adult life. The world, my world, was in chaos. Two years later, when I turned eighteen, the Vietnam War was beginning to evolve into something huge and scary. The media was all over it and there was talk of drafting massive numbers of young men to fight in Vietnam. Though I had planned to leave Tennessee after high school and bum around Europe where I hoped to find myself, perhaps in some of the cafés frequented by Sartre and Hemingway, I enrolled in the local university for no other reason than to avoid the draft, but the draft board drafted me anyway. I was assigned to the Army Security Agency, the elite military arm of the National Security Agency and principal intelligence unit of the Army, and six months after being inducted into the Army I found myself at the Tan Son Nhut Air Base in Vietnam, just outside Saigon.

Finding myself in Vietnam I felt even more resentful, desperate, and alone than I had been in Tennessee. My wish to get out of Tennessee had come true, but as Truman Capote once cautioned, beware of answered prayers. Along with all my cohorts at the 509th Radio Research Group, the thinly disguised intelligence base masquerading as a pool of clerk typists, I was convinced that fate had taken me to Vietnam for a reason: to die. I was convinced I would never live to see the US again and that all the anguish I had suffered the past five years was a presage to where I now found myself, in a war no one believed in, against an enemy no one understood. I set about preparing for death by reading everything I could get my hands on. This was when I first encountered Nietzsche, Camus, Kafka, and Heidegger, all sent to me by my family in Tennessee. In this most existential of places I readily embraced this tragic sense of life that Sartre, Nietzsche, and Kafka articulated so vividly. I found this strangely comforting, and I am certain it was what got me through that year, counting each day toward the magic number 365 when perhaps, by the intervention of some miracle, I might return state side. Though I couldn't believe I would really make it, I couldn't stop myself hoping that I would. In spite of all my cynicism and self-doubt, my desire to live and carve out a life for myself persisted, stronger than ever. I believed I had my existentialist bedfellows to thank for that.

Those years, from fourteen to nineteen, were pivotal for me and shaped the direction I was to follow when I finally returned home from Vietnam. What I realized once our plane touched down to safety was that the *Angst* I had experienced in Vietnam wasn't specific to a war zone, where one's life is literally on the line. By now my *Angst* had become a constant companion, and I realized that this *Angst* is a constant in life, and a friend, not an enemy. I had decided at the ripe age of twenty that I was going to become a psychoanalyst and devote myself to engaging others in the same kind of dialogues that Socrates had, thereby tying my twin passions together, philosophy and therapy. The coalescence of all these factors, my ejection from Cuba via revolution, the search for meaning in small town Tennessee, the catastrophic loss of my mother, the alarm and sense of doom that occasioned the Cuban Missile Crisis, my abduction from college by my own government to the Red Zone of Vietnam, all these had made existential philosophy my religion, and my deliverance.

After separating from military service I moved to San Francisco to resume college and to study psychology. In 1970 psychology was all the rage in America and San Francisco was ground zero for all the interesting things that were happening in that field. LSD, yoga, Buddhism, meditation, City Lights Book Store in North Beach, the center of the Beat generation's writers and poets, including Ken Kesey, Jack Kerouac, Lawrence Ferlinghetti, sex, drugs, rock and roll, the Jefferson Airplane, the Grateful Dead. It was all happening. From the ridiculous to the sublime, from the hell of Tennessee and Vietnam to the utopia of San Francisco, I felt I had earned it, maybe even deserved it. Yet, hippy San Francisco was an intellectual wasteland and psychology, despite all the hip accouterments and bell bottom trousers, was, ultimately, superficial to me. Psychoanalysis was in retreat and you had to be careful who you told that you read Freud. To my dismay, there was no Heidegger on the curriculum, no Sartre, no Nietzsche. In those days, anyone interested in integrating existentialism and psychoanalysis had to make do with a collection of essays by mostly German and French psychiatrists who struggled to adapt the philosophy of Martin Heidegger into their psychodynamic perspective, led by two Swiss analysts, Ludwig Binswanger (1963) and Medard Boss (1963). [4] These efforts were so mind-numbing and esoteric that it was impossible to detect any element of an existential sensibility in their work. Then R. D. Laing entered the picture.

I hadn't discovered Laing until I moved to California when, walking along Muir Beach a few miles north of San Francisco in Marin County, I struck up a conversation with an interesting stranger about philosophy and my interest in Sartre. The young man unceremoniously pulled out a paperback copy of *The Divided Self* from his backpack and handed it to me, to keep. "Here," he says, "I think you're going to like this." I never saw that love child again, but this kind of generosity wasn't unusual in 1970s San Francisco. In the following two years I read everything Laing had published and became obsessed with his thinking and way of articulating the incredibly dense ideas he had such an easy facility with. In the autumn of 1972 Laing paid a visit to Berkeley on a national lecture tour that billed him as "The Philosopher of Madness." Seeing him in person and then meeting him after his lecture was all the encouragement I needed to leave graduate school and move to London, in order to study with him in 1973.

In the early 1970s there really was no place to train as an existential psychoanalyst except for Laing's Philadelphia Association in London. That was pretty much it. Much has changed since the 1970s. In that decade, Laing had become the most famous and widely read psychiatrist in the world. Much of this was due to his publications, including *The Divided Self* (1960 [1969]), *Self and Others* (1961 [1969]), *The Politics of Experience* (1967), *The Politics of the Family* (1971), and many others. These books not only integrated existential philosophy and psychoanalysis, they were a breath of fresh air, written in a lively and engaging style that was compelling. Students, like myself, came to London from North America and Europe to train with him and he did not disappoint them. By 1980, the year I returned to San Francisco, other training programs began to emerge, adding to other schools already in existence that had offered other, non-psychoanalytic approaches to integrating existentialism with psychotherapy, including the Medard Boss institute in Zurich (Daseinsanalytic Institute), and Logotherapy Institutes scattered throughout Europe and South America, founded by Viktor Frankl. These included a degree program at Regents College in London, founded by Emmy van Deurzen and Ernesto Spinelli, and the Existential-Humanistic Institute in San Francisco, founded by Kirk Schneider, a former student of Rollo May. Another student of Rollo May, Irvin Yalom, began to write books on existential psychotherapy that got a wide press and elevated him to a position of renown in the emerging interest in existential therapy, though Yalom was not affiliated with any training programs. What linked all of these clinicians who were identified with various conceptions of an existential based approach to psychotherapy was that none of them, save for Rollo May, were psychoanalysts. Indeed, they were to varying degree hostile to psychoanalysis, with the exception of

Yalom whose mentor, Rollo May, was a trained psychoanalyst and a close friend of R. D. Laing. Yet, even Rollo May's many publications (by the 1970s May and Laing were the two most famous existential practitioners in the world) demonstrated no hint of psychoanalytic thinking, opting to shun psychoanalytic nomenclature from his writings. Indeed, May once confided in me that his psychoanalytic training and subsequent association with the Alanson While Institute, founded by Harry Stack Sullivan, was a frustrating affair because the Institute, known for its conception of *interpersonal* psychoanalysis, was not remotely interested in May's efforts to bring existential philosophy into their curriculum. It was no doubt for this reason that May chose to go out on his own, so to speak, left New York for San Francisco, and make no mention of his psychoanalytic background in his numerous publications. He was subsequently regarded, not as an existential psychoanalyst, but as an existentialist *psychologist*, which then became his professional identity. Though May enjoyed his share of private students, and established an affiliation with Saybrook Institute in San Francisco, he was never again affiliated with a training institute.

Similarly, his student, Irvin Yalom, adopted some of May's psychodynamic perspective — for which he has been roundly criticized by the British existential therapists and "analysts" — but like May references virtually no psychoanalysts in his writings nor any of its core concepts. Yes, May and Yalom are more psychodynamic than any of the other existential therapists, humanistic or otherwise, but take pains to distance themselves from psychoanalysis as a discipline. A properly existential psychoanalysis must be rooted in *psychoanalysis*, not some vague reference to "psychodynamic" principles.

Existential THERAPY Versus Existential PSYCHOANALYSIS

So, what is the difference between an explicitly existential *psychoanalysis* and all the other schools that fall loosely under the rubric existential *therapy*? The very first psychiatrists and psychoanalysts who sought to integrate psychoanalysis with the philosophy of

Martin Heidegger were Ludwig Binswanger and Medard Boss, both Swiss psychiatrists who were affiliated with their fellow Swiss psychiatrist, C. G. Jung, located in Zurich, and his then-colleague, Sigmund Freud, located in Vienna. Binswanger and Boss trained with each, taking far more from Freud than from Jung. Each had different ideas of how such a merger of the two disciplines might work. Binswanger named his therapy existential analysis (not *psycho*analysis, a term reserved for followers of Freud), yet he was so indebted to Freud that contemporary existential therapists accuse Binswanger of having been far too indebted to Freud, despite Binswanger's aim to replace Freud's theories with those of Heidegger. Like Boss, Binswanger (1963) was more invested in *correcting* Freud's conceptions of the unconscious and transference phenomena than he was in *integrating* them into his notion of existential analysis. Similarly, Boss devoted a book, *Psychoanalysis and Daseinsanalysis* (1963) (daseinsanalysis was the term Boss adopted for his brand of existential therapy, alluding to Heidegger), with the aim of translating Freud's basic theories into a less "psychoanalytic" nomenclature.

The results were mixed at best, burdened with a nomenclature far most impenetrable than even the worst of Freud's terminology. The fact is that Freud was an exemplary and accomplished author, blessed with that rare ability to make complex ideas clear and inviting. This unfortunately was not the case for either Binswanger or Boss. They did however succeed in introducing Heidegger into the language of psychiatry, and a legion of other European psychiatrists, mostly French and German, employed this new language into their assessment of the human condition. These writers inspired a newer generation, including R. D. Laing and Rollo May, to employ existential theories into their own publications. A new generation of psychiatrists and psychoanalysts were introduced to these ideas after the publication of a volume of papers written by Boss, Binswanger, Minkowski, and several other European existential therapists, edited by Rollo May, Ernest Angel, and H. F. Ellenberger, titled *Existence: A New Dimension in Psychiatry and Psychology* (1958). The 1960s and 1970s were dominated by translations of European existential practitioners into English as well as the emergence of new American journals, such as the *Journal of Existential Psychiatry and*

Psychology, devoted to this new school of psychotherapy. Many if not most of these early converts to existential therapy were psychoanalysts, including Fritz Pearls.

By the 1980s, nearly all of these practitioners from both the first and second generations of existential practitioners had died, save for Laing and May. And by this time a new generation of existential therapists had emerged, virtually none of them psychoanalysts. Instead, this new generation, including the so-called *British School of Existential Analysis* (Emmy van Deurzen, Ernesto Spinelli), various chapters of the *Logotherapy Institute* (Viktor Frankl), the *Existential-Humanistic Institute* in San Francisco (Kirk Schneider), the *Boulder Psychotherapy Institute* (Betty Cannon), and my *New School for Existential Psychoanalysis* (founded in 1988, under the rubric of *Free Association, Inc.*) in San Francisco, were actively engaged in introducing psychotherapists to existential philosophy. Among those actively training and educating existential therapists who were not affiliated with an institute, were Rollo May, Irvin Yalom, Ludwig Lefebre, Walter Menrath, and Julius Heuscher, all located in San Francisco. Virtually all of these groups, save for Free Association, Inc., were and are hostile to psychoanalysis, to varying degrees. None employ the term psychoanalysis in their nomenclature.

It goes without saying that all of these groups and institutes comprise exemplary thinkers and therapists, all influenced by existential philosophers and ideas. They provide excellent therapy or they would not flourish. Nor am I suggesting that existential psychoanalysis is inherently better, or more effective or user-friendly, or in any way superior to a form of psychoanalysis that is not rooted in an existentialist sensibility. So what are the distinguishing factors that separate existential psychoanalysis from all the other non-psychodynamic existential therapies? In asking this question, we are perhaps also asking what distinguishes *psychoanalysis* from non-psychoanalytic therapies?

I will begin with a few words about what distinguishes *existential* psychoanalysis from conventional schools of psychoanalysis. There are two distinguishing features of existential psychoanalysis that set it apart from all the other schools of psychoanalysis. First, existential psychoanalysis is the most *personally engaged* form of psychoanalysis, epitomized by its lack of technique. Second, any existential approach to psychoanalysis must first and foremost be explicitly *concerned with the human condition*: why do we suffer, why is our mortality a principal concern, and how can we come to terms with the fundamental role that suffering plays in our lives? Existential psychoanalysis not only dispenses with technique. There is no intrinsic underlying theory that applies to existential psychoanalysis. Similar to the Middle School of psychoanalysis, each existentialist is obliged to fashion his or her own theoretical perspective. However, each approach to existential psychoanalysis, whoever the practitioner happens to be, must be fundamentally rooted in *existential philosophy*. It is up to each practitioner to determine which existential philosopher or philosophers they choose to privilege. Similarly, it is up to each practitioner to decide which psychoanalyst (or psychoanalysts) they wed their vision of psychoanalysis to, whether that analyst is Freud, or Winnicott, or Bion, or Lacan, or Laing, or whoever. I happen to privilege Sigmund Freud and R. D. Laing, and I will show in this introduction to existential psychoanalysis why I regard Freud as the very first existential psychoanalyst, due to his emphasis on the human condition, on the relation between suffering and psychopathology, on his indebtedness to Plato and Aristotle as the source of his understanding of the human condition, as well as the source of Freud's skeptical orientation, and finally on Freud's emphasis on the role that love — and its absence — plays in our suffering, as well as in our recovery.

In distinguishing existential psychoanalysis from non-psychodynamic existential therapies, there are three fundamental differences worth noting. First, existential therapies reject the psychoanalytic conception of the unconscious. They tend to conceive of the unconscious as a *second subject*, lurking somewhere beneath consciousness, that determines our conscious motives and actions. While it is true that this does describe the way that most psychoanalysts characterize this concept, I have shown elsewhere (2024, pp. 171–205) that there is no such thing as an "unconscious," but rather that we are, for the most part, unaware of the motives that guide us most of the time, and that this is perfectly natural. It is only a problem when we are ambivalent about our desires, and are of two minds about what we want, and the anxieties that our desires naturally arouse.

Second, following their rejection of unconscious processes, existential therapies also reject the psychoanalytic conception of *transference*, the notion that we are constantly projecting aspects of earlier relationships onto current ones, especially our therapists. Because such transferences are unconscious, which is to say we are not aware of them, existential therapists reject this notion for the same reason they reject the concept of unconscious processes.

And third, existential therapies tend to reject the phenomenon of diagnosis, a term borrowed from medicine and applied to psychological phenomena. This is a complicated issue and I could not agree more that Freud's conception of diagnostic categories, both adopted and adapted by subsequent schools of psychoanalysis, should not be taken literally, but metaphorically. When Freud, for example, talks about neuroses and psychoses, he is not referring to a medical condition or diagnosis, but a way of trying to understand the myriad ways that we protect ourselves from our fears and anxieties by suppressing or denying them. I could not agree more with the view that the psychiatric bible of diagnostic categories, the *Diagnostic and Statistical Manual* (volumes 1 through 5), is utter nonsense, created for the sole purpose of determining which psychotropic drugs are best suited for the psychological symptoms psychiatric patients are experiencing. Indeed, I wrote a book, *The Death of Desire: An Existential Study in Sanity and Madness*, to offer an alternative way of treating the very concept of "psychopathology" (2017).[5] In my view, it is important to distinguish between milder neurotic symptoms and more serious psychotic ones when determining whether one feels qualified to accept a given patient into therapy.

For these reasons, existential therapists do not tend to diagnose, yet they also tend to shy away from working with patients suffering from psychotic and schizophrenic symptoms! In my view, psychoanalytically trained therapists are better equipped to work with severely disturbed patients than non-psychoanalytically trained therapists, whether those therapists are existentially oriented or not.

The following chapters are intended to explore these questions in more depth, with the aim of articulating the features of a truly existential psychoanalysis, in contrast to other schools of psychoanalysis and existential therapy. I know thus far I have not provided a perfectly crafted encapsulation of what the term *existential* means. I have alluded to it, and perhaps that is the only authentic way of approaching the matter, by allusion. I hope I have at least provided an appetizer, a taste of more to come. The rest of this book will be drawing from a variety of existential thinkers, and I will try my best to explain how I wed each to the psychoanalytic tradition, indeed how psychoanalysis, in its latency, *has always been* existential, in the manner that I conceive the term. There is no existential theory, nor an existential technique, for there is not nor can there be anything remotely resembling an existential "how to" by the numbers. Given its inchoate nature, existentialism, and any derivative approach to therapy, can never be articulated from a theoretical perspective that will meet with universal agreement. This is why existential psychoanalysis can only ever be rooted in a *sensibility* which, in turn, is based on a manner of being with another person.

When all is said and done, the existentialist sensibility is nothing more or less than a style of engagement that is at once personal and elusive, that haunts every moment of the time we allot ourselves to engage in that most mysterious and perplexing of callings, the therapeutic process. I now turn my attention to the first person who coined the term *existential psychoanalysis*, Jean-Paul Sartre.

Notes

1 From the film, *Blade Runner*, based on Dick's novel, *Do Androids Dream of Electric Sheep?*
2 For a more complete treatment of the skeptic tradition see my essay, "The Sceptic Dimension to Psychoanalysis: Toward an Ethic of Experience" in Thompson, 2000.
3 I see certain features of the twentieth-century existential tradition as having derived from Sigmund Freud. For more see my *The Truth About Freud's Technique* (1994).
4 See also May et al., 1958.
5 In fact, R. D. Laing's first two books, *The Divided Self* (1960 [1969]) and *Self and Others* (1961 [1969]) were existential studies offering alternate way of understanding the concepts of diagnosis and psychopathology from an existential perspective.

References

Binswanger, L. (1963) *Being-in-the-world: Selected papers of Ludwig Binswanger* (J. Needleman, trans.). New York: Basic Books.

Boss, M. (1963) *Psychoanalysis and daseinsanalysis* (L. Lefebre, trans.). New York: Basic Books.

Freud, S. (1953–1973) *The standard edition of the complete psychological works of Sigmund Freud*, 24 volumes (J. Strachey, ed. and trans.). London: Hogarth Press. (Referred to in other references throughout the book as *Standard edition*.)

Freud, S. (1905 [1953]) *Three essays on the theory of sexuality*. In *Standard edition*, 7: 125–245. London: Hogarth Press.

Heidegger, M. (1927 [1962]) *Being and time* (J. Macquarrie and E. Robinson, trans.). New York: Harper and Row.

Kierkegaard, S. (1980) *The sickness unto death: A Christian psychological exposition for upbuilding and awakening* (H. Hong and E. Hong, eds. and trans.). Princeton, NJ: Princeton University Press.

Laing, R. D. 1960 [1969]) *The divided self*. New York and London: Penguin Books.

Laing, R. D. (1961 [1969]) *Self and others*. New York and London: Penguin Books.

Laing, R. D. (1967 [1983]) *The politics of experience*. New York: Pantheon Books.

Laing, R. D. (1982) *The voice of experience*. New York: Pantheon Books.

May, R., Angel, E., and Ellenberger, H. (Eds.) (1958) *Existence: A new dimension in psychiatry and psychology* (various translators). New York: Basic Books.

San Juan de la Cruz (2003) *The dark night of the soul* (E. A. Peers, trans.). New York: Dover Publications.

Sartre, J.-P. (1943 [1954]) *Being and nothingness* (H. Barnes, trans.). New York: Philosophical Library.

Sartre, J.-P. (1962) *Sketch for a theory of the emotions* (P. Mairet, trans.). London: Methuen and Co.

Sartre, J.-P. (1964) *Nausea* (L. Alexander, trans.). New York: New Directions.

Thompson, M. G. (1994) *The truth about Freud's technique: The encounter with the real*. New York and London: New York University Press.

Thompson, M. G. (2000) The sceptic dimension to psychoanalysis: toward an ethic of experience. *Contemporary Psychoanalysis*, Volume 36, No. 3: 457–481.

Thompson, M. G. (2017) *The death of desire: An existential study in sanity and madness* (2nd ed.). London and New York: Routledge.

Thompson, M. G. (2024) *Essays in existential psychoanalysis: On the primacy of authenticity.* London and New York: Routledge.

Chapter 2

Sartre and Psychoanalysis

The relationship between psychoanalysis and existentialism has always been an uneasy one, for myriad reasons. The antipathy between psychoanalysis and philosophy generally is undeniable, typically delineated on the frontier between the science of the unconscious, on the one extremity, and the science of consciousness, on the other. From there misunderstandings and snap judgments explode. Instead of obvious collaboration, we get competition and vitriol. And then there are the existential philosophers. Who can understand them? Though many existentialist thinkers are cited among the few psychoanalysts who read them, those that have had the most radical impact are Fredrich Nietzsche, Martin Heidegger, and Jean-Paul Sartre. Sartre enjoys the distinction of being the first person to coin the notion of an existential psychoanalysis and devoted several chapters in his magnum opus, *Being and Nothingness*, to delineating its features.

Sartre's relationship with psychoanalysis is broad, for Sartre had a lot to say about it in multiple contexts. My relationship with Sartre and psychoanalysis is complex and deeply personal. I discovered Sartre in my teens, the perfect age, looking back, to make his acquaintance. As I noted in the previous chapter, I grew up in Cuba in the 1950s, where my father, an American entrepreneur and chemical engineer, became friends with Ernest Hemingway, among the few American expatriates living on the island. I was fond of Hemingway, and remember him mentioning his friend, Sartre, who was about to visit Cuba with Simone de Beauvoir after Castro seized power. Hemingway thought that Sartre was

DOI: 10.4324/9781003595427-2

something of a shit, the epitome of the French intellectuals that Hemingway got to know when living in Paris in the 1920s. But he admired Sartre's writing, as well as his celebrity, and most of all he admired his fame and his success. Though Sartre was not awarded the Nobel Prize for literature until after Hemingway's death (which Hemingway had won in 1954), they were bonded by Hemingway's impact on French writing, including Sartre's, and their mutual admiration. They were both non-conformists, and they each insisted that the only way to live is authentically, no matter the cost. One of the things I admired most about Hemingway was that he knew how to *live*. He loved the life he was living, and treated it as an adventure. Hemingway and Sartre were, as my Irish grandmother once suggested, a pair to draw to.

I was too young to read Sartre then, but a few years later, after my family had abandoned Cuba for their native Tennessee, I checked him out. Sartre introduced me to existential philosophy, and it became a sort of religion for me, if a secular one. This was also around the time I discovered Sigmund Freud, and I formed this unconventional idea that Sartre and Freud were saying the same thing, but in different languages. In the years that followed, I managed to get through Sartre's early philosophical works, but it was the section devoted to existential psychoanalysis in *Being and Nothingness* that riveted my attention. By the time I graduated from high school, I had decided I was going to become an existential psychoanalyst — whatever that was.

Life has a funny way of throwing us a curveball now and then. Without warning, Tennessee drafted me into the Army and sent me to Vietnam, in the summer of 1966. Like many of my compatriots there, I was convinced I was sent there to die. I was lucky, however, to be assigned to an intelligence unit in Saigon, and this afforded me the luxury of reading in my off time. I dove into Sartre and Nietzsche. They taught me that we are always dying, that the closer we get to death, the more precious life becomes. I think Sartre especially helped me live my death, and survive it, and for that I will always be grateful.

After I separated from the Army, I moved to San Francisco to study psychology. That was when I discovered R. D. Laing, the Scottish psychiatrist and existential psychoanalyst. By 1970 Laing was the most famous psychiatrist in the world, due to his bestselling books and his groundbreaking work with schizophrenia. I was soon on my way to London, having abandoned my graduate studies, in order to work with him.

Like me, Laing was passionate about Sartre. One may even read Laing's classic, *The Divided Self*, as an integration of Sartre's philosophy and object relations theory. This was unusual. Nearly all the psychiatrists who were drawn to existential philosophy after World War II embraced Heidegger, not Sartre. Perhaps this was because so many of them were German-speaking psychiatrists, or because they were captivated by Heidegger's impenetrable prose. Or they may have been put off by Sartre, the bad boy of existential philosophy. Perhaps worst of all, Sartre was a Frenchman!

I think what bonded me to Laing was that we had both discovered Sartre in our youth, in the throes of rebelliousness, and were each drawn to his contempt for everything *bourgeois* and conventional. This attitude is not typical of people who choose to enter the so-called mental health professions. As a class, I would characterize my colleagues as unremittingly conventional, uncommonly anxious, and materialistic social climbers. I know this sounds harsh, even petty, and I don't mean it to sound that way. Some of my best friends are psychoanalysts. I love them despite their relatively narrow conception of psychoanalysis. But this is the kind of observation that Sartre inspired, perhaps the reason why few of my colleagues gravitated to him. Like Sartre, I have never been materialistic, perhaps to a fault.

What I want to talk about here, however, is Sartre's relationship with Freud, epitomized by his critique of psychoanalysis in *Being and Nothingness*. Freud, too, was a bad boy, a trouble-maker, and undeniably obsessed with sex. This was probably what drew me to him as a teenager. Sartre and Freud: *another* pair to draw to. So here I am, in the company of the three bad boys of the twentieth-century *avant-guard*: Sartre, Laing, Freud. I was in heaven.

So what is the relation between Sartre and psychoanalysis? Perhaps some of you are already familiar with what he says about this in *Being and Nothingness* (which I strongly urge you to read, if you have not), but if you aren't we will have to save that for another day. For now, I want to focus on how Sartre's thinking transformed psychoanalysis into a truly human, which is to say inherently personal, way of engaging clinical practice. In order to do this I will explore three topics that are basic to understanding the essential elements of existential psychoanalysis, as I conceive it. The first concerns Freud's conception of the *unconscious*. The second is Sartre's conception of *freedom*, and the role it plays in existential psychoanalysis. And third, what do we make of the concept of *change*? How does this come about? And what, exactly, do we mean by this term?

Freud's Conception of Psychic Reality

Let's begin with Freud's theory of the unconscious, and the problems this concept continues to engender. Freud's first topography for demarcating a distinction between conscious and unconscious aspects of the mind concerned the nature of fantasy and the role it plays in neurosis. After he experimented with and subsequently rejected hypnotism Freud surmised that each person is preoccupied with two kinds of fantasies: one I am aware of and the other I am not. Freud opted to label those that I am not aware of "unconscious," because we have no reflective experience of them. These so-called unconscious fantasies have been repressed, and are inaccessible to us, but because they still reside "in" the unconscious portion of our minds they engender psychic *conflict*, which manifests in our dream life as well as our psychopathology, including neuroses and psychoses.

Freud's first, topographical, model of the unconscious was simple: one portion of the mind is conscious and the thoughts it contains are in the forefront of awareness (i.e., *reflective experience*), whereas another portion of the mind is unconscious and composed of fantasies that I am not aware of. Freud also included a third element in this topography, the preconscious, which contains unconscious — or non-conscious — thoughts and memories that can be recollected at will. Freud's topographical model served as a map of what he terms "psychic reality." Freud's depiction of psychic reality is necessarily contrasted with *factual* reality, which is investigated by the empirical sciences and readily available for study.

Yet, in what sense can one treat fantasies as "realities" when, after all, they are not real? Freud recognized that fantasies can be *experienced* as real in a similar way that objective reality is experienced. In other words, fantasies, though not literal depictions of the past, nevertheless convey meaning, and such meanings are capable of telling us more about our patients than the so-called facts of their history. By *interpreting* both fantasies and their consequent symptoms as meaningful, Freud was able to obtain truths about his patients that were otherwise hidden. His opposition between psychic and external realities served to juxtapose an inherently personal reality with a concrete one. This isn't to say that concrete, or objective, reality is necessarily false, but it was Freud's genius to see that the truth about one's history can be derived from the communication of otherwise innocuous reflections, by interpreting a patient's fantasies as disguised messages. The recognition that fantasies could be conceived as messages suggested there was something concealed in them that the patient neither recognized nor understood.

This means that fantasies serve a purpose: they disclose the intentional structure of our deepest longings and aspirations. *They tell us what we desire.* But Freud lacked a conception of intentionality that could explain how his patients were able to convey the truths they didn't "know" in a disguised and indirect manner. In other words, his patients *unconsciously intended* their symptoms and the attendant fantasies that explained them — they weren't "caused" by their unconscious. Yet, Freud seemed conflicted as to the origin of such symptoms. He never entirely abandoned the idea that they must be *caused* by some traumatic something or other, a notion more popular today than ever. If not external reality, then perhaps they originate in the vicissitudes of our unconscious fantasy life?

Despite the recent development of relational psychoanalysis, which claims to approach the treatment relationship from a more interpersonal perspective, contemporary psychoanalysts, with few exceptions, find it agreeable to use terms in which *impersonal* aspects of the unconscious predominate. Analysts remain wedded to the notion that non-personal facets of the mind account for the unconscious motives that guide us in our daily affairs, which in turn produce our so-called psychopathology.

Sartre's Critique of the Unconscious

Whereas Freud depicted psychoanalysis as a science of the *unconscious*, it is impossible to deny that it is also a science — if we can call it that — which is preoccupied with *consciousness*, if only implicitly. Terms like truth, epistemology, knowledge, understanding, and comprehension pervade every psychoanalytic paper that is devoted to the unconscious as a concept. This is also the subject matter that Sartre, Merleau-Ponty, Heidegger, and Ricoeur devoted a considerable amount of their philosophical writings to: What is the nature of knowledge and what role does it serve in our everyday lives? Of all the phenomenologists, it was Sartre who took psychoanalysis the most seriously, even conceiving his own brand of "existential psychoanalysis" (1981).

In Sartre's critique of psychoanalysis (1962, pp. 48–55; 1981, pp. 153–171) he rejected Freud's topographical model for similar reasons that Freud eventually did so himself. In the topographical model the only thing separating the system-conscious from the system-unconscious is the so-called "censor," which, according to Freud, regulates what is permitted into consciousness and, contrariwise, what is repressed into the unconscious. This means that the censor is aware of everything, that which is conscious and unconscious alike. Yet because the ego is *unaware* of the censor, this model posits a *second* consciousness (the censor) that is both unknown and unknowable to the ego. Sartre's problem with this model is obvious: the so-called censor is the *de facto* "person" who is being analyzed and disclaims knowledge of all the shenanigans he employs in order to disguise what he is up to, an edition of what Sartre terms "bad faith," or inauthenticity. Freud also had problems with the implications of a "second thinking subject," and decided to discard this model for one that contained only one subject that *knows* — the conscious portion of the ego — and substitute in its place not one, but three subjects that do not know anything: the id, the superego, and the unconscious portion of the ego (which employs defense mechanisms, such as repression, denial, projection, etc.).

Freud's subsequent revision of his earlier model, however, fares little better in Sartre's opinion. The topographical model is replaced with one that is less concerned with demarcating conscious and unconscious portions of the psyche than with determining the complex nature of psychic agency, or subjectivity. Sartre's complaint with the new model is that it still fails to resolve the problem of *bad faith*, the problem of a "lie without a liar." If anything, the new model gets even further away from Sartre's efforts to *personalize* the unconscious, by instituting three psychic agencies that protect the conscious portion of the ego from any responsibility for its actions. *How would Sartre propose to remedy this situation, to account for those actions that Freud claimed the "conscious" patient is "unconscious" of devising, while holding the conscious patient responsible for performing them?*

Sartre accomplishes this by introducing two sets of critical distinctions into the prevailing psychoanalytic vocabulary. The first is a distinction between pre-reflective consciousness and reflective consciousness, and the second is between consciousness and knowledge. Sartre summarizes the basic dilemma in Freud's conception of the unconscious with the following questions: How can the subject not know that he is possessed of a feeling or sentiment that he is in possession of? And, if the unconscious is just another word for *consciousness* (Sartre's position), how can the subject not know what he is *de facto* conscious of? Sartre's thesis of pre-reflective consciousness is his effort to solve this riddle. Following Husserl, Sartre saw consciousness as *intentional*, which means it is always conscious *of* something. This means there is no such thing as empty consciousness; nor is there such a thing as a container or receptacle that houses consciousness. Instead, consciousness is always outside itself and "in" the things that constitute it as consciousness-*of* something. In Sartre's (1957) words:

> Intentionality is not the way in which a subject tries to make "contact" with an object that exists beside it. *Intentionality is what makes up the very subjectivity of subjects.*
>
> (pp. 48–49) [emphasis in original]

In other words, the concept of intentionality renders subjectivity as already a *theory of intersubjectivity*, since to *be* a subject is to be engaged with some thing "other" than one's self — even if this other something is merely an idea. Sartre elaborates how this thesis would be applied to the social world in this famous passage:

> When I run after a streetcar, when I look at the time, when I am absorbed in contemplating a portrait, there is no *I* (or "ego"). There is [only] consciousness *of the streetcar-having-to-be-overtaken*, etc … In fact, I am then plunged into the world of objects; it is *they* which constitute the unity of my consciousness; it is *they* which present themselves with values, with attractive and repellent qualities — but *me* — I have disappeared; I have annihilated myself [in the moment of conscious apprehension].
>
> (1957, pp. 48–49)

This means that when I experience a rock, a tree, a feeling of sadness, or the object of my desire in the bedroom, I experience them just where they are: beside a hill, on the meadow, in my heart, in relation to myself and my beloved. Consciousness and the object-of-consciousness are given at one stroke. These things constitute my consciousness of them just as I constitute their existence *as* things through the act by which I perceive them and give them a name. And because naming things is a purely human activity, these things do not exist as rocks, trees, or emotions in the absence of a human consciousness that can define them through the constitutive power of language.

Yet, such acts of naming don't necessarily imply *knowledge* of what I am conscious of. This is because Sartre distinguishes between the pre-reflective apprehension of an object and our reflective "witnessing" of the act. Ordinarily when I am pre-reflectively conscious of a feeling, for example, I intuit the feeling of sadness and, in turn, reflectively acknowledge this feeling *as* sadness: I feel sad and experience myself as a sad person simultaneously. But I am also capable of feeling sadness, or anger, or envy, without *knowing* I am sad, or angry, or envious. When this is suggested to me by my analyst I am surprised by this observation. Initially, I may resist my analyst's interpretation and reject it. But I may eventually come to admit it because, once brought to my attention, I am also capable, upon reflection, of recognizing that this feeling is *mine*. Sartre argues that I would be incapable of recognizing thoughts or ideas that I claim no awareness of *unless I had been conscious of these feelings in the first place, on a pre-reflective level*. Though conscious, the pre-reflective isn't *known*. According to Sartre, it is *lived*.

In other words, what Freud labels consciousness Sartre designates reflective consciousness (i.e., knowing *that* I am conscious of this or that), and what Freud labels the unconscious (but not the preconscious) Sartre designates as that moment of pre-reflective consciousness that, due to *bad faith*, has not yet yielded to reflective awareness and, with that awareness, knowledge of it. This is why I can be conscious of something that I have no immediate knowledge of, and why I can become knowledgeable about something that I am, so to speak, "unconscious" of, but am subsequently able to discover. This implies that I can only actually *experience* something I have knowledge of, but not what I am only pre-reflectively conscious of. It is this inherently existential reading of the unconscious that non-psychoanalytic existential therapists don't get.

The difference between Sartre's and Freud's respective formulations isn't that it merely substitutes Freud's terminology with Sartre's. On a more radical level it eliminates a need for the notion of a second thinking subject *behind* or beneath consciousness, and offers a way to personalize the unconscious in a manner that eluded Freud.

Sartre and Emotions

I now want to review Sartre's critique of the emotions, and his transformation of a psychoanalysis rooted in psychology to one rooted in existential phenomenology. First I want to ask, what *are* emotions? There is no shortage of theories that try to tackle this problem, yet with no consensus on a definition. For some emotions are distinct from cognition and judgment, while for others our feelings are central to decision making and even determine our judgments. It is undeniable that emotions tell us things that our cognitions often miss. Moreover, emotions are often the driving force behind our motivations, whether positive or negative.

And what about the relationship between emotion and desire? Are emotions derived from desires, or are they determinant? Whatever they are, we cannot deny that we would not be human without them.

The term emotion dates back to 1579 when it was adapted from the French *émouvoir*, meaning "to stir up." It was first introduced to academic circles to replace a similar term, passion. Though the two terms have often been used interchangeably, passion is typically employed when referring to sexual feelings. There is also the problem with their respective etymology. Passion derives from the Latin *pati*, meaning to suffer or endure. One can see why the term passion began to take on different connotations than when simply feeling this or that. The French *émouvoir* appeared to solve the problem. Like the term, feeling, with which emotion is used synonymously, an emotion is of brief duration, whereas moods last longer. The more recent "affect," adopted by psychoanalysis, encompasses all three. It is also the root of the word, affection.

Psychoanalysis went a long way in explaining how human behavior is not orchestrated by random events, because actions always have a motive, an intention, a specific end, even if we are ignorant of what the end is. Psychoanalysts were the first to emphasize the *significance* of psychic phenomena, that this seemingly innocent thought or emotion often stands for something else. The child who steals from his mother's purse is only trying to reclaim the mother's love. A girl who faints at the sight of parsley can't bring herself to recall a painful childhood incident when she was forced to eat vegetables. Yet, often as not, the psychoanalytic interpretation, if only surreptitiously, tends to privilege causal antecedents masquerading as interpretations in order to explain pathogenic behavior. History plays a crucial role in our lives, and this is just as true for people suffering from emotional disturbance. This is why I can project onto all women the quality of withholding because my mother was too depressed to comfort my needs. Each time I feel attracted to a woman, I find myself consumed with ambivalence, fear, consternation, and excessive devotion. The feelings I experience in these situations not only color my understanding of reality. To a significant degree, they determine *who I am*.

Freud's term for that traumatic moment every child is supposed to experience is the *Oedipus* complex. What makes this complex so compelling is the sense of betrayal that occasions it, feelings that every boy or girl must eventually come to terms with. I cannot say whether Sartre was influenced by Freud's dark assessment that love plays in our lives. Their respective views on the matter are remarkably similar, and form the basis of Sartre's many plays and novels.

Emotions may be pleasing or painful. The pleasurable kind we don't question until they become self-destructive, but even then we rarely oppose them. The painful variety are more invasive and problematic. Because they elicit distress, we can bear them for only so long. Like Jason clutching the Medusa, we divert our eyes and conceal our experience of them with magic, what Freud termed defense mechanisms. Our emotional life, always a mystery to us, inhabits a spectrum between desire and anxiety, each feeding the other. If we are creatures of our desires, and anxiety is the price we pay for them, then emotions must be entangled inside those desires in principle. Emotions are not merely barometers that tell me when my desires are satisfied or thwarted. They also possess an intelligence of their own that aims to make my life as agreeable as possible. That's not all. My emotions also shelter me from realities that are too painful to stomach. Sartre suggested that emotions are our way of magically transforming a situation we get stuck in, like a fly on a sticky-mat, that we can neither accommodate nor escape. In other words, emotions provide a way of escaping situations that would otherwise drive me crazy. According to Sartre:

> When the paths before us become too difficult, or when we cannot see our way, we can no longer put up with such an exacting and difficult world. All ways are barred and nevertheless we must act. So then we try to change the world; that is, to live it as though the relation between things and their potentialities were not governed by deterministic processes, but by magic.
>
> (1962, p. 63)

The woman who faints at the sight of her attacker does so not because it reminds her of some previous event, but because it removes her, albeit magically, from the present situation. She no longer has to face the immediate danger she is in. But this isn't to say she willfully faints with deliberation. She is seized by the situation, a situation that makes demands on her and with which she is unable to cope. Or rather, her manner of coping is so ingenious that it is unrecognizable as such to the unwary observer. The unlikelihood of finding a solution to the problem she faces demands that she invent a solution instead. If she can't take flight in reality, she can do so emotionally, which is to say, magically. Yet an emotional response isn't just a substitute for other kinds of action, other ways of coping, because it isn't effectual. It doesn't act on the world but merely changes my perception of it.

On a more basic level, the emotion is a structure of desire. It may be a way of enhancing a desire I enjoy, or a way of coping with a desire that is too risky, a desire that elicits fear. The person in danger wants to be somewhere else, so the fainting magically fulfills the wish to vanish. Similarly, if I want something I cannot have, my emotions can help remove the desire itself, allowing me to evade a disappointment. Sartre invokes the sour grapes analogy as a common rationalization for this strategy.

Sartre's purpose in his early phenomenological study, *Sketch for a Theory of the Emotions* (1962), was to show why behaviorism is incapable of explaining the phenomenon of emotions, because behaviorism is stuck in a cause-and-effect universe that cannot account for the *intentional structure* of our motives, our folly, our madness. Psychoanalysis goes further because it is sensitive to human agency, but then ascribes our motivations to "unconscious" responses to trauma that, if we aren't careful, may be just as causal as behaviorism. At its best, what is often lacking in the psychoanalytic explanation is the personal dimension to motives, because unconscious motives are not, according to most psychoanalysts, strictly speaking personal, so we cannot take responsible for them.

Freedom and Choice

So what are therapy patients supposed to make of this? How are they supposed to effect change in their lives? Isn't this the purpose of therapy: to change our manner of being in the world, and improve it? How can this happen without turning the therapeutic situation into a *technology*? The essential task of existential psychoanalysis as envisioned by Sartre is hermeneutic, that is, deciphering the meaning of acts in relation to a synthetic totality underpinned by an original project of being, manifested in a fundamental choice. But what is choice, exactly? We ordinarily speak of choice as a volitional, deliberate act that is transparent to itself. This suggests that we are always ahead of our choices, that we weigh them in our minds and, having decided upon this or that option, execute them. Sartre is even sometimes accused of adopting this model, but it isn't that simple.

Say I want to go to the cinema. Which movie do I choose to go see? I look at the options and pick this one over the other. There! I have deliberated, weighed my options, and chosen the one most desirable. Or have I? One of the things that both Freud and Sartre share in common is that neither buys this explanation. Though separated by an enormous gulf in theory, temperament, and vocation, each concluded, as did Heidegger, that choices are free, but not willful. Instead, they are predetermined. Something or other *predisposed* me into making that choice. Freud would say I did so unconsciously, whereas Sartre would argue that the choice occurred on a pre-reflective level. In both cases, it wasn't my ego or "I" that chose the action. The choice executed was rendered before the fact, beneath awareness, in my engagement with the world. The so-called *conscious* choice merely makes it official, after the fact. I wanted to see this movie but didn't know it, until it simply "occurred" to me.

In other words, I cannot get ahead of my choices, I am always one step behind, as they guide me this way or that, so the choices themselves, and the reasons I make them, are often puzzling, but not necessarily unpleasant. This is why psychoanalysis, as envisioned by Freud, is always retrospective, not prophylactic. Only in behavioral psychology do we play the fiction of deliberating what we intend to do, and then execute the act. In psychoanalysis, the idea is to review *previous* actions, and to learn something about ourselves from them. The actions reviewed may be buried in our childhoods, or they may have occurred moments earlier, in the analytic session. In either case, we are not talking about an executive function, but a *reflective* one.

This has led some commentators to conclude that Freud's conception of the unconscious was deterministic. If we don't make our choices "consciously," which is to say, *volunteeristically*, then our choices must be made *for* us — by our unconscious. This implies that there is no free choice in the matter, if my choices aren't willfully executed. Psychoanalysts make this assumption because the unconscious is supposed to be *impersonal*, not personal. In Freud's tri-partite structure, it isn't "me" guiding my decisions, but the *id* (Latin for "it"). This is the crux of Sartre's problem with the psychoanalytic conception of the unconscious, the problem of a lie without a liar, a thought without a thinker, an action without an actor.

What is at stake here is our notion of the self, what comprises the self, and how free the self is. For Sartre, there is no self, so to speak, no "I," not even a subject, if by subject we mean some sort of entity that, like the censor, orchestrates our lives via executive decision making.

Unlike Freud, Sartre roots the person, not in psychology, but in *situation*, in the world to which we belong, the world where we live and die. All of my choices derive from my engagement with that world, not in my psychology. That doesn't mean that I am determined by that engagement. I *am* that engagement. I have choices in the matter, and those choices are free, but that doesn't mean I am in control of the situation, or the choices I make. The fact that my choices are free doesn't make me Superman. Freedom doesn't make me omnipotent. It isn't a freedom to rule, but a freedom to be me, and to ultimately embrace the me that I am.

This means that my choices are ontological rather than deliberate. Sartre suggests our neuroses go all the way back to a fundamental choice, in childhood, when we chose what our neurosis would be, on a pre-reflective level. In other words, we *intend* our psychopathology, we are not the consequence of this or that trauma. Contrary to behaviorism, or even psychoanalysis, nothing *caused* my condition. Rather, I *chose* to experience this or that incident *as* traumatic. And I continue to complain about that trauma as a source of comfort.

Given this thesis, how is therapy even possible? If I cannot will myself to health, then how does it come about? As Kierkegaard would say, through indirection. In this context, all my conscious, knowing mind is good for is to acquaint myself with the mystery of my existence and to plummet its depths, over an unpredictable amount of time. I cannot will myself to overcome my fear of intimacy. I cannot compel myself to love more fully, behave more compassionately, or feel more alive. Yet, all of these transitions may and often do result from the analytic endeavor. How? We don't know, exactly. All we do know is that knowing oneself has the potential to change our lives in this way, to become who we are, authentically. If we are intrepid, over time, this process of self-reflection may result in a change of perspective, and with it, a change in our selves, which is to say, our lives.

This can only happen indirectly, over time, *without ever knowing that we have made these changes until after having made them* — and without ever knowing why.

This is where authenticity comes into the picture. When I tell myself I hate the person I am, that I cannot give up my addictions, that I wish I could be more this or less of that, I am lying to myself. Because every choice I make is a free choice, and because everything that I am is a consequence of the choices I have rendered — and I know you will find this hard to believe — I am always the person I wish to be. To be in conflict with myself is to pretend that something or other has "caused" me to be this way — something other than my free choice to be this way. This is inauthenticity, or bad faith, in its essence.

This also means that the goal of existential psychoanalysis is to become the person I am already, unreservedly, wholeheartedly, passionately, not ambivalently or reluctantly. This is not an ethical endeavor, to make me a "better person." I don't know if Sartre would agree with this, but it seems to me this form of radical self-acceptance that it aspires to is an act of love. It entails falling in love with the person I am and always have been, the same person who lived this life, and suffered its folly, up to this very moment in time. At the end of the day, existential psychoanalysis is nothing more, or less, than a cure through love.

Conclusion

In conclusion, how has this perspective affected my way of working with psychoanalytic patients? I think, like perhaps all analytic practitioners, I assumed early in my career, going back some forty years or so, that the therapeutic enterprise was all about change. This word has always haunted me. I remember thinking that I wanted to tackle this problem head-on, and to write a book about change, what it is, how it is effected, and so on. I abandoned this project once I realized that the very concept of change is problematic. We don't even know what it is. It was only later, when I had absorbed some insights from the existential philosophical tradition, that I finally came to realize that psychoanalysis isn't about change, but rather becoming. Change implies that something that was should be discarded and replaced with something else. This works fine in the physical universe, where we readily change one flat tire for a new one, a house we no longer cherish for one more desirable, and so on. But you don't discard the person you are for a new, improved model. You are stuck with who you are, for better or worse, for life. This is when it came to me that we are always becoming, but not, strictly speaking, changing. In becoming, we are always what and who we are, but we are never finally that person until the end, until the day we die. As long as we live we are constantly evolving. This is why we are constantly, ceaselessly, becoming more and more ourselves. But this becoming isn't a panacea.

Without reflection, without care, and without concerted effort to reflect on our situation, we very well may simply become more and more miserable instead, more and more alienated from ourselves in order to escape the anguish of living. Existential psychoanalysis provides an opportunity to become something different than that. It offers the opportunity, with no guarantees, to become more and more the magnificent creature that we can be, the person that, in our hearts, we already are. Once on the road to becoming and embracing ourselves, we have a chance to be at peace with ourselves, even to celebrate ourselves and the lives we have led up to this point. When we are finally at peace with ourselves, we are at peace with the world. As Sartre would say, we are finally able to *exist*.

I now turn to the most cardinal principle of existential psychoanalysis, epitomized by the term *authenticity*. As essential to existentialism as the unconscious is to psychoanalysis, I hope to show how the goal of a properly existential conception of psychoanalysis can never be concerned with a medicalized (or even psychologized) relief of *mental illness*, but rather to become, at the most basic level, who we are.

References

Sartre, J.-P. (1957) *The transcendence of the ego* (F. Williams and R. Kirkpatrick, trans.). New York: Noonday Press.

Sartre, J.-P. (1962) *Sketch for a theory of the emotions* (P. Mairet, trans.). London: Methuen and Co.

Sartre, J.-P. (1981) *Existential psychoanalysis* (H. Barnes, trans.). Washington, DC: Regnary Gateway.

Chapter 3

Vicissitudes of Authenticity

One of the prevailing themes that has haunted the psychoanalytic discourse from its inception is the basis of the analytic relationship and the nature of the uneasy dialogue between analyst and patient. Whereas Freud characterized this discourse as one that both requires and enhances a unique capacity for honesty, I have increasingly found it more useful to characterize this relationship in terms of a quest for authenticity, a project that was first articulated by existentialist philosophers. Even when authenticity is not explicitly invoked by the person who aspires to it — which is usually the case in psychoanalysis — analytic patients and practitioners alike nevertheless allude to authenticity in the way they oftentimes characterize the goals of treatment and the demands that are made on both participants in the analyst–patient relationship.

Though authenticity is not a technical term in any conventional psychoanalytic text with which I am familiar, the idea of what I take authenticity to mean has pervaded psychoanalysis from its inception. For example, when Freud (Breuer and Freud, 1893–1895 [1955], p. 305) suggested that the goal of analysis is to "transform hysterical misery into common unhappiness," he was invoking authenticity as an essential, if undeniably ambiguous, goal of psychoanalysis. Similarly, when Winnicott (1989, p. 199) argued that "If we are successful [as analysts] we enable our patients to abandon invulnerability and become a sufferer," he was addressing the analysand's capacity to accept the inescapable reality of suffering and the need to embrace such suffering honestly,

DOI: 10.4324/9781003595427-3

or authentically. And when Bion (1974, p. 13) says that whenever analyst and patient meet together that both of them should be experiencing fear and that, if they are not, they have no business being there, he was also invoking authenticity as an inevitable presence in every analytic encounter. Neither Freud nor Winnicott nor Bion, of course, employ authenticity in their writing, but the sense of it pervades the corpus of their respective psychoanalytic sensibilities.

So why hasn't the term authenticity been incorporated in a more explicit way into the psychoanalytic discourse? I'm not sure I can provide a convincing answer to that question, as I continue to be puzzled by it myself. Of course, we know that authenticity was first employed as a concept by existential philosophers, not psychoanalytic practitioners. Though its sensibility can be traced back to Nietzsche and Kierkegaard, it was Heidegger who first coined the term and made it the backbone of his philosophical perspective. The term was subsequently adopted by other existentialist philosophers and soon after by psychoanalysts who became identified with the existential perspective. Ludwig Binswanger (1963), Medard Boss (1963), and R. D. Laing (1969) are only some of the many psychoanalysts who came to epitomize an explicitly existentialist approach to psychoanalysis in Europe, whereas in America mainstream analysts such as Hans Loewald (1980) and Stan Leavy (1980, 1988) were profoundly influenced by the writings of Heidegger. In recent years, other terms that were originally identified with existential psychoanalysis, e.g., hermeneutics, intersubjectivity, and social constructivism, have filtered into the American psychoanalytic milieu, and authenticity has even been invoked in the recent contemporary relational literature (e.g., Mitchell, 1992). Yet none of the American analysts who have adopted these ideas would call themselves existentialists and few of the Europeans who preceded them are cited in the psychoanalytic literature. There remains a profound cultural divide between European and American sensibilities when it comes to articulating the ends of the analytic treatment experience and it appears that the concept of authenticity occupies an uneasy role at the interface between them. For example, European cultures tend to view suffering as a source of strength and character whereas

American culture tends to view suffering as a source of trauma and psychopathology.

Though there are contemporary and popularized versions of authenticity that reduce it to feeling states and forms of moral behavior (Taylor, 1991), for the purposes of this chapter I restrict the concept to three elementary attributes: 1) that it furthers behavior that is inherently *unconventional* or pertains to the road less traveled; 2) that it is the more difficult or *arduous* path and consequently more rewarding in a way that the less onerous path is often not; and 3) that it is *genuine*, but in a way that resists generalization because it is context-specific and consistent, for example, with efforts in the psychoanalytic literature to characterize aspects of the extra-transference relationship as *real* or honest, with a concomitant absence of subterfuge or contrivance. What I am suggesting is that authentic relating has always been a hallmark for the way that some psychoanalysts conceive the nature of their clinical practice, but not all. And of those who do meet this criterion (e.g., Freud, Bion, Winnicott, Lacan) their relationship with the concept of authenticity has been implicit, not necessarily explicit.

I divide this chapter into four sections. In the first I review the concept of authenticity in Nietzsche and Heidegger; in the second I discuss the principles in Freud's treatment philosophy that are consistent with authenticity, including free association, neutrality, and abstinence; in the third I explore the relationship between authenticity and the role of suffering in the work of Winnicott, Bion, and Lacan; and in the fourth I examine the role of authenticity in the so-called transference and countertransference relationship, specifically the real and genuine relationship in the analyst–patient interaction. I conclude with a brief discussion about the role of courage in the analytic situation.

I Authenticity in Nietzsche and Heidegger

Though Heidegger was the first philosopher to employ authenticity as a technical term, both Nietzsche and Kierkegaard were important sources for this feature of Heidegger's philosophy. For Nietzsche (2002, 2003), authenticity characterized the person who is not afraid to face up to the fundamental anxieties of living. He saw this ideal person as one who would emerge one day in the future capable of "overcoming" the difficulties that his generation, Nietzsche believed, was incapable of facing up to. This special individual was embodied in Nietzsche's conception of the *Übermensch*, usually translated into English as a super-man or more literally, "overman," a person who would come to grips with her fears and in that sense overcome the weight of her existence by accepting reality for what it is, unbowed and unafraid. Nietzsche rejected the Enlightenment view that society is in an inexorable process of evolution that will inevitably improve from one generation to the next with scientific breakthroughs that will make our lives more satisfying and countered that in many respects our lives are actually getting worse, due to the alienation that technology often occasions. In Nietzsche's opinion, our capacity to reason is not as objectively reliable as Enlightenment philosophers claimed, because humans are driven by passion, the source of which is predominantly unconscious. Nietzsche's *Übermensch* would be capable of recognizing this observation and possess the necessary courage to face it (Thompson, 2004d).

There are other qualities that the *Übermensch* embodies that are just as consistent with Nietzsche's rejection of contemporary society, including: 1) an opposition to authority that results in a fierce individualism; 2) a concerted skepticism that rejects absolute truths of any kind, embodied in Nietzsche's pronouncement that *God is dead*; 3) a perspectivism which holds that truth is wedded to the perspective of the person who promotes it, not by fixed, immutable standards; and finally, 4) a moral relativism which holds that all truths are relative to a time and place and, so, neither eternal or objective but intrinsically personal and fluid.

So how does Nietzsche's conception of the *Übermensch* compare with Heidegger's notion of authenticity? Though Nietzsche's philosophy had a profound impact on Heidegger, one would be a mistaken to construe Heidegger's authentic individual as nothing more than a twentieth-century edition of Nietzsche's *Übermensch*. One of the principal differences between Nietzsche's *Übermensch* and Heidegger's conception of authenticity is that for Heidegger there is no such person who epitomizes an "authentic hero" in juxtaposition to less endowed neurotics. Instead, authenticity is characterized by Heidegger as a specific act or moment in any individual's life where the context in which a situation arises offers opportunities to behave authentically or not. Unlike Nietzsche, Heidegger rejected the notion of an ideal person who would someday emerge to replace the stereotypical contemporary neurotic; an idea he thought was stuck in a modernist way of thinking. Heidegger argued that all humans are essentially inauthentic in their being, because the nature of social relationships is such that we necessarily compromise with others in order to get along, and because we love them. But sometimes in order to sustain such relationships we get along with others so well that we neglect our own needs, but pretend to ourselves that we are doing no such thing, or that we cannot afford to be upsetting, or "difficult," and concern ourselves with security to such a degree that we deny the very things we are most passionate about.

In order to understand what authenticity properly entails it may be helpful to ponder what it means to be inauthentic. In Heidegger's magnum opus, *Being and Time* (1962), he characterized inauthenticity as an incidence of "fallenness" (*Verfallenheit*), as when a person sells out to the others' expectations in order to curry favor. A preoccupying theme throughout Heidegger's work was the relationship between the individual and society and how it engenders a conflict that we can never entirely resolve. This is because we humans are existentially isolated and in our loneliness crave the comfort of feeling at one with others, not unlike the *Oceanic* experience that Freud describes in *Civilization and Its Discontents* (1930 [1961]). For Heidegger and Nietzsche alike, this sense of belonging is an illusion. Though this quest is inconsolable, says Heidegger, the only way of approximating this feeling is by abandoning an essential aspect of what we are about, our personal integrity. Yet, if we are condemned to be inauthentic as a basic feature of our character, how can we also be granted a choice in the matter, to choose *not* to be so on certain occasions? This is the kind of conflict that bedevils many marriages.

The distinguishing feature of the so-called true artist contrasted with the pretensions of commercial artists rests precisely on the notion that the real article is authentic, that the work this artist is faithful to is a truth that is generated from somewhere "within," from an inner core of his or her being that cannot be accessed by skill or training, but rather some indefinable trial of suffering, *Angst*, or unique something or other that belongs to this artist and none other. By this reckoning, we don't have to rely on Rousseau's or Descartes' conception of a tangible self, whether real or inner, in order to render the notion of the contemporary artist as we have come to know him as legitimate. On the contrary, the artist has helped *us* learn something about the nature of authenticity itself, irrespective of which theory of the self (de-decentered or otherwise) we are partial to.

Whereas Socrates and Plato offered what is arguably the first notion of authenticity rooted in a self that knows who it is by achieving a kind of wisdom that derives from self-knowledge, the Greek skeptics advocated a method for overcoming the need to acquire such knowledge in the first place, treating such quests as symptoms of, should we say, an obsessional neurosis (Groarke, 1990). Instead of a knowing self, the skeptics envisioned an *experiencing* self that is capable of submitting to the world *as it is given*, in all its mystery and ambiguity. By suspending judgment about my ability to predict the outcome of events as they occur from one day to the next, the skeptic learns not to comprehend his experience in order to surmount it, but to *suffer* it in order to accept it, and be with it. The skeptics believed if you can overcome your obsessive quest for knowledge — including self-knowledge — a transformation in consciousness may occur, a kind of releasement or giving-way that they claimed is relatively free from worry, a constituent of living authentically.

One of the areas of contention among postmodernist thinkers regarding authenticity is the problem of the self, or subjectivity, which postmodernism rejects. As we have seen, popular literature on authenticity, going all the way back to Rousseau and the Romantics, situates authenticity in the notion of a feeling-self that is a version of the Cartesian ego, but in place of an ego that is based exclusively on rationality, the Romantics preferred a self that is imbued with feeling-states instead. In either case, the notion of a reified self that is substantial and constant results in the idea of a hidden or true self that lies beneath an outer or social self, so this conception of authenticity degenerates into a private kernel of a self that is "inside" oneself, so to speak, and to varying degrees unconscious. While this conception of authenticity has been adopted by popular culture and American humanistic authors, it was summarily rejected by both Nietzsche and Heidegger. In fact, a great deal of Heidegger's efforts were devoted to addressing the problem of the self and how to conceive of authenticity without recourse to the notion of a substantial or reified — in a word, subjective — self.

Heidegger argued that we live our lives in an everyday sort of way without thinking about what we are doing and, more importantly, without having to think our way through our activities as a matter of course. The place he assigned to reason is an after-the-fact operation that is not primary to our engagement with the world, but secondary. It is only when our involvement with the world breaks down that we take the time to momentarily withdraw from it in order to ponder what just happened and why. According to Zahavi (2001), "At the beginning of his analysis of *Being and Time* Heidegger writes that a subject is never given without a world and without others. Thus ... it is within the context of [every human being's] being-in-the-world that we come across intersubjectivity" (p. 124).

Whereas Husserl begins with the individual's relationship with oneself and goes from there to others, Heidegger begins with our relationships with others and then sets out to investigate how to determine, or reclaim, our relationship with our selves (Thompson, 2001c). In other words, we dwell within a common public "totality of surroundings" that constitute us as individuals, in a world *from* which all of our perceptions, sensibilities, and experiences derive. We are not principally occupied with perceptual objects in a remote and theoretical way, but rather with handling, using, and taking care of things in a manner that does *not* rely on our cognition (awareness) of what we are doing *at the moment* we are doing it. Heidegger is at such pains to emphasize the primordial structure of our being-with the world before we ever become individual subjects that he coins a new term for depicting each human being's essential status as a being. So instead of using the familiar terms subject, ego, or self, he uses the German

Dasein, which has no English equivalent. The literal English translation would be there-being or the more common, being-there, a cumbersome and unsatisfactory rendition compared with what some translators have rendered as the more colloquial *existence*. This is also misleading because, after all, we are still talking about a *person*.

Basically, Heidegger is drawing a distinction between what we typically depict as the subject or self, which, in his view, are constructs, from a more fundamental way in which we exist in the world primordially. "I" exist first and foremost as a being of the world from which I cannot extricate myself very easily. The person I take myself to be is essentially an invention that I have a hand in creating, but the greater part of my self's authorship derives from what others make of me. In fact, I am so obsessed with how others see me that I want to make myself into the person they expect me to be and, to a significant degree, that is who I am in their company. Moreover, who I take myself to be is not just rooted in the past. "I" am also constantly in the making and becoming, every waking moment of my life. In Heidegger's view, we never really overcome this condition and are always looking to "them" to tell us what we should do and whom we must become in order to be loved and acceptable.

This doesn't suggest that Heidegger ignores the past; it is just as crucial to him as it was to Freud, but for Heidegger the past is co-existent with the future to which I aim because I am always trying to correct perceived inefficiencies from my past life with possibilities I perceive ahead of me. Most of the time I feel to varying degrees "thrown" into a maelstrom of competing notions that others have a hand in constructing the person I take my "self" to be. To make matters even more complicated, others are not everybody else but me, a totality from which I stand apart. Instead, "they" are me also, but from whom I do not customarily distinguish myself. Dasein — this matrix in which I constantly dwell without necessarily ever knowing it — is something that can be, and usually is, *others*. Yet in everyday life we do not ordinarily experience our "selves," nor do we ordinarily experience "others" — in fact, for the most part we are incapable of telling the difference between the two. According to Zahavi (2001):

We do not experience ourselves in contradistinction to some sort of inaccessible foreign subjects; rather, our being-with-one-another is characterized by replaceability and interchangeability. We are there in the world together with others [so that] the "who" of the Dasein who is living in everydayness is therefore anyone, it is *they*.

(p. 130)

From a Heideggerian perspective, the problem of empathy with which Husserl was so preoccupied — the problem of how an isolated subject can ever make contact with others — is a moot issue because we are with others in our primoridality to such an extent that we can never escape them. This is why my absorption in the world has the character of being lost, not in a desert but amongst others, in search of the self I genuinely am or can become. This is because I (or rather Dasein) do not possess a self-identity on which I rely, nor can I. Instead I have to appropriate myself and because of this, once having done so can just as easily lose myself again, and eventually do, over and over again. Dasein's self, which is always in the making, can never be an objectively constituted entity, the culmination, one might wish, of a "thorough" analysis, but only as a *manner of existing*.

So if Heidegger's conception of authenticity is rooted in a rough and ready notion of a self that is inherently insubstantial, that lacks fixed characteristics and exists in a state of yearning towards a future that it never reaches, then how can the essence of such a self be conceived, even when it is couched in this mysterious context that Heidegger calls Dasein? Whereas postmodernists tend to view the self as a fragmented collection of episodic states of semi-consciousness that is constructed by the social and cultural forces constantly working on it, including economics, sex, politics, fashion, and media, Heidegger sees all of these elements as important influences, but none as important as the power that language has over our self-identity. Moreover, and perhaps even more importantly, we aren't merely shaped by language passively, like robots; we also *have a hand* in our relationship with the words that constitute our being and the kind of person we turn out to be. If my history plays a decisive role in the person I am, I also play a role in changing my history, adding to it, and arriving at new understandings of it through new interpretations of it every time I revisit and think about it. My past and my self are never fixed — they are alive to change and revision as long as I am capable of giving thought to the circumstances my life is rooted in.

The function of language, from this viewpoint, is to tell stories, which we engage in every time we communicate with each other. From a narrativist perspective, the self is not a static entity, like a character in a book whose personality is fixed in the mind of its author. It is instead a continuous, never-ending story that has no culmination until the moment of death, so our stories have this open-ended quality to them that defies clearly defined boundaries. Although this produces anxiety in each of us, it also elicits a sense of wonder and possibility, without which our lives would be unimaginable, and boring. It is this very sense of wonder that the psychoanalyst capitalizes on in the analytic process by utilizing language to discover approximately who the person being analyzed *is*, by reflecting on the significance of the communication patterns that spontaneously come to mind in the course of the open-ended conversations shared between them.

But if my self is so insubstantial, if I am what I take myself to be in that moment that I wrest my identity from an inauthentic they that competes with me at every turn to determine who I am for me; and if I have the freedom — the responsibility, even — to revisit my previous interpretations of myself with fresh eyes and perspectives in order to detect the fallacy of previously undetected corruptions in my earlier self-definitions, then what, ultimately, does anyone have to hang the hat of his or her self-identity on? What's to stop me from just changing my mind — and my self — at every whim and convenience whenever it suits me to do so? What's to stop me, in the name of authenticity, from giving myself over to a form of unbridled narcissism that surreptitiously seeks the easy way out at every turn, but does so in the name of authentic "unpredictability"? One of the German words that Heidegger employs for authenticity in *Being and Time* is *eigentlich*, which comes from the root meaning "own." Heidegger sees the authentic act as one in which I appropriate from the myriad of influences that I am constantly subjected to in my world and my history, that which I (choose to) make "my own." Character traits, attitudes, opinions, and what have you become identified with who I take myself to be, not because of some reasoned argument, but arbitrarily and unconsciously. But due to my powers of reflection I am also able to survey these choices and in a secondary sort of way decide whether I want to commit myself to them and *become* them, until such a time that I choose to revise them anew. The point Heidegger is trying to articulate is that the committed person, which is to say, the authentic individual, takes such choices seriously and views them in terms of building a structure or, in the vernacular of his later work, a temple to his or her relationship with being. As such, *who* each person is becomes something of a tradition and the seeds of a destiny that can be counted on, what we in America would call a person of substance or character.

Now all this may sound suspiciously narcissistic — and potentially criminal — to the person who is looking for evidence of a concept of authenticity that is tied to a standard of moral virtue that meets acceptable social mores, which, after all, is precisely what morality implies.[1] Postmodernists reject authenticity because they reject any pretension to a socially sanctioned code of ethics that can be imposed on any individual, which they mistakenly assume that all theories of authenticity embrace. Like Nietzsche, Heidegger was opposed to the idea that society has the right to impose such standards willy-nilly except in the form of laws that are legislated and adjudicated in the courts, but he wasn't opposed to the idea of *virtue* in principle. The problem comes down to who gets to decide what virtue is and which virtues one should hold as most important, how religiously they should be applied and how allowing we should be of individual imperfections. Remember that for Heidegger we are essentially *inauthentic*, fallen creatures and that authentic selfhood is the exception, not the rule. Moreover, Heidegger refused to link authentic choices with ethical ones. Because ethics is a product of our relationships with others, we first need a standard for our relationship with our *selves*, however insubstantial and inherently narcissistic the self may be. The concept of authenticity is intended to meet this standard. So when push comes to shove, how do we know when we are choosing authentically and when we are taking the easy way out? How can we tell when we are in touch with our ownmost being and when we are deluding ourselves with an act of momentary convenience? Can a person be authentic and selfish at the same time?

As you might expect, Heidegger's answer to this problem is not so easy to grasp. It comes down to the observation that the authentic choice is never the easy one, but always the road less traveled. If I am going to trust my conscience to be my guide, the inherent anguish that authentic choices entail should be a reliable if not perfect foil to the selfishness that more crippling editions of narcissism often engender, yet consistent with the "destining" that Heidegger associates with authentic moments of significance. Contrary to the postmodernist who rejects values in principle because they can never be universalized, the authentic person embraces values, however arbitrarily and subjectively chosen they may be. And even if my values are different from yours, those values are nevertheless my own and an integral part of my authentic self-identity. They speak to who I *am*. In the end, because the self is insubstantial, the only thing I have to hold onto is what I make of myself. So the person I call my self stands for and represents a tradition I have become and that I will continue to foster and tinker with for as long as I live. Certain views and character traits become precious simply because they are *mine*, because they are now part of this strange and indefinable, yet indispensable "me." While I can always change who I am, the important thing is to determine whom, of all the people I can be, I decide to commit myself to.

All this comes down to living with an awful lot of anxiety about who I am, why I do the things I do, and what I can possibly do to change the person I am when the person I have become is miserable. Both Nietzsche and Heidegger saw anxiety as a necessary and inevitable accompaniment to acting authentically. We are anxious due to a pervasive sense of alienation, the starkness of which is captured by Nietzsche's declaration that God is dead, or has abandoned us — meaning that in the postmodern era in which we live there are no universal values to which we can cling and the ground we walk on is no longer as solid as we once assumed. In Heidegger's phrase, we are thrown into a world that is not of our choosing, but we are nonetheless obliged to decide who we will be by virtue of the choices we make, even if our so-called choices are for the most part unconscious. This leaves us feeling alone in our decisions and the world we live in, so we try to mitigate our anxiety by complying with what we imagine others want from us. The inauthentic individual, like the neurotic, eventually discovers that compliance never meets with the kind of reward she longs for, yet she finds the alternative — the isolation of being her own person, come hell or high water — equally untenable.

If, as Heidegger proposes, it is impossible to know from one moment to the next what our motivations are, and whose motives we are, in fact, serving at a given moment, then it isn't difficult to see why this conception of authenticity would be so troubling to conventional morality. If no one can set definitive standards for what authenticity entails, then how can we ever know whether we are being true to our selves or just acting from a convoluted strategy of compliance, on the one extreme, or a not-so-subtle form of conventional narcissism on the other? This is the question I want to turn to next by reviewing those aspects of authenticity that are readily evident in psychoanalysis.

II Authenticity in the Work of Sigmund Freud

In order to appreciate the importance of authenticity in Freud's treatment perspective we should first examine his presuppositions about the nature of suffering and the role it plays in our lives. This topic is important because analysts and patients alike go into the treatment situation with their own views about what suffering entails and how much of it we can expect to diminish. There's no denying that Freud's take on the human condition is unconventional by contemporary North American standards. This is largely because it was born from a European, post-World War I, existential perspective that is anathema to the typical American mindset. Whereas in this country psychoanalysis was enthusiastically embraced as a tool of psychiatry in its never-ending war on mental illness, in Vienna and other European capitals such as Berlin, Paris, and London, psychoanalysis was marginalized by psychiatry and became a refuge for artists, writers, and intellectuals — and anyone wealthy enough to pay for a six-times-a-week analysis. Many of Freud's patients came to see analysis as a means of facing the harsh realities of living instead of a device for the simple relief of their symptoms.

Yet, this paradox presented Freud's patients — most of whom came to him from all over the world — with a quandary: Everyone goes into analysis in the first place because they suffer and want their suffering to diminish. In fact, without the motivation to sacrifice whatever it takes to effect a change in one's condition, the prospective analytic patient, Freud advised, should be refused treatment. Since the beginning of Western thought, philosophers, physicians, and religious leaders have been concerned with the nature of suffering, its ostensible causes, and its elusive relief. From earliest times we have sought to understand what our suffering is about and how to relieve, accommodate, or accept it. Freud, though trained as a physician, was never willing to accept the strictly medical approach to suffering: To relieve it by any means possible, whatever the cost. Freud knew from personal experience that *life entails suffering*. The patients he treated suffered miserably, yet seemed peculiarly intolerant of it. Because their desire for happiness caused them frustration, they instinctively suppressed those desires they believed occasioned their suffering. How could psychoanalysis help them? Whatever kind of anguish analysis is suitable for relieving, Freud soon realized it could not be expected to relieve the kinds of suffering that life inevitably entails. This is because life subjects us to suffering. Life, in turn, eases the burden of suffering with momentary respites of pleasure and the promise of fleeting, if not lasting happiness. In Freud's opinion we are only capable of experiencing happiness in the first place because we suffer, but we compound our suffering even more when we crave happiness to unreasonable extremes. How can any person be expected to come to terms with this equation, which by its nature entails more suffering, not less?

In his most popular work, *Civilization and Its Discontents* (1930 [1961]), Freud argued that neurotics find this equation unacceptable because they feel, to varying degrees, that life is systematically thwarting them. They grow to resent their suffering and become increasingly desperate to rise above it. In their haste to relieve suffering, however, they overlook what their anguish is telling them. They become so preoccupied with diminishing their unhappiness they forget that if you reduce life to simply relieving your misery you become so obsessed with it that the relief you seek becomes increasingly elusive. These were the kind of people Freud wanted to help, but the way he decided to help them wasn't by diminishing their suffering, but by increasing it, in Zen-like fashion!

Freud knew that if the patients he treated had any chance of success, he would have to reeducate them about the role that suffering plays in our lives. Taking from Aristotle, Freud believed that every human action is in pursuit of the good, but the problem lies in each person's conception of the good, and such conceptions can serve us well or lead us to ruin. So which conception of the good did Aristotle advocate? Aristotle believed that the good life should be equated with the pursuit of happiness, but he also observed that, for most people, pleasure is the focus of their lives and, consequently, how they conceive happiness. Aristotle believed there was a good far nobler — and in the end, more reliable — than pleasure, which is virtue, not because virtue serves utilitarian aims (such as relief from suffering), but because virtue is its own reward. In other words, whereas most people pursue happiness by means of accruing wealth and pursuing pleasurable activities, Aristotle argued that people of poor character will always be miserable while those of good character will be rewarded for it. Consequently, the virtuous person is happy — at any rate *with him/herself* — while the person who pursues only pleasures is always in danger of losing them and is consequently plagued with anxiety, i.e., naked fear.

And what is the highest virtue? According to Aristotle, honesty — the capacity to be honest with others but, more importantly, the capacity to be honest, more authentic, with oneself. Freud's problem was in persuading his patients to follow this counsel to the degree that it could make a difference in their lives. Like Aristotle, Freud believed that the capacity for honesty hinges on the strength of character each person is capable of developing. So the first thing every analyst must learn is that you don't build character by conceiving of ways to relieve suffering, but by developing the strength to bear it. This makes the outcome of analysis and the drama that occasion's the inevitable termination ambiguous, and sometimes tragic. This is because the kind of suffering analysis is capable of relieving isn't the pain of suffering, specifically, but the alienation we experience when we know that the life we are living is a lie. The ability to overcome this lie, by becoming more honest with ourselves, can relieve the alienation, but not the anguish that the slings and arrows of misfortune exact from us.

It should be clear by now that the standard Freud is using for the outcome of analysis is far more complicated than the simple reduction of symptoms that we have become all too well accustomed to in the rhetoric of contemporary psychobabble. In fact, Freud is talking about something most people probably don't ordinarily equate with relief from mental distress, but something along the lines of character building, or personal integrity. What is peculiar to analysis is its singular approach to suffering, embodied in the rule of abstinence and the so-called classical technique: *a certain quota of suffering should be endured in order to accrue the full benefit of what analysis can offer*. While psychoanalysts have always experimented with *relaxing* this aspect of their treatment regimen, they have never opted to entirely abandon it, so the question comes down to how much suffering are we talking about? What kind of suffering does psychoanalysis subject us to? And what are the varieties of contexts in which analytic patients are expected to encounter such suffering and accommodate it?

I now want to focus on three components of psychoanalytic practice — Freud called them technical recommendations, not *rules* — that are especially evocative of authenticity, the three technical principles that most poignantly characterize Freud's treatment philosophy: 1) the fundamental rule of analysis, i.e., the patient's acts of self-disclosure; 2) the rule of neutrality, i.e., the analyst's capacity for non-judgmental open-mindedness; and 3) the rule of abstinence, i.e., the patient's capacity to suffer. These three principles are hardly exhaustive. Most of the technical recommendations of psychoanalysis, including the use of countertransference and the admonition against therapeutic ambition, are concerned with authenticity, but I will focus on the first three for now.

The fundamental rule is a contract — explicit or implicit — that analytic patients are introduced to in the early stages of analysis. Freud called this contract a pledge or a promise, so when patients agree to free associate they essentially promise to do so. (Let's leave aside for the moment whether this pledge is explicit or merely implied, which is nowadays more typically the case.) On the other hand, the *act* of free associating is not a pledge but a spontaneous form of conversation in which patients are invited to participate by being unreservedly candid. To freely associate in the manner that Freud intended requires nothing more complicated than the willingness to speak spontaneously and unreservedly, as we sometimes do when not the least self-conscious about what we are disclosing to another person. But in this case the stakes are so high that a considerable amount of anxiety is expected. Obviously, Freud's conception of free association doesn't make much sense unless we appreciate the degree to which we ordinarily conceal most of what spontaneously comes to mind in the course of ordinary conversations.

Free association is not, however, so much a *process* as a form of verbal meditation that entails speaking unreservedly while remaining attentive to what we are disclosing, something we do not ordinarily do. Most of us either speak impulsively without awareness of what we say, or we think through everything we are about to disclose before speaking. This is because patients instinctively want to censor things about themselves that they believe will lead the analyst to judge or dislike them. As we know, it takes a lot of courage to disclose things about ourselves that we customarily hide, no matter how open-minded an analyst purports to be with his or her patient.

Yet, simply disclosing things about ourselves doesn't necessarily entail an authentic way of being. We may be "honest" in the strict definition of the word by verbalizing everything that comes to mind, but not always in a fashion that is consistent with authenticity — in a manner that is heartfelt, considered, risky. The one isn't always or necessarily the same as the other. Freud was aware that some patients are content with engaging in a kind of verbal diarrhea by disclosing virtually nothing of significance, though technically "honest." What makes free associating potentially authentic is the way each of us faces the risk of exposing things about ourselves — to our analyst as well as to ourselves — that we are ambivalent about disclosing. This is because, as Nietzsche observed, once our secrets are exposed they change our perception of ourselves and the core of who we take ourselves to be. We may regret having said something and want to take it back, but we can't. Once uttered, we have ingrained a piece of ourselves onto the fabric of the world for all to see, embodied in our relationship with our analyst. The analyst bears witness to our confessions and admissions, and however spontaneous and unconsciously intended they may be, they are no less revealing.

Similarly, the rule of neutrality speaks to the analyst's capacity to be just as authentic with her patients as her patients are trying to be with her. One of neutrality's most salient features was Freud's counsel to adopt a mode of evenly suspended attentiveness that is probably more familiar to practitioners of Buddhist meditation than to scientifically trained psychologists. For example, Freud advised analysts against trying to *remember* everything that patients tell them because by the very act of trying to they select what they think is important instead of giving everything equal weight. This is challenging to do because the most difficult thing analysts usually encounter is how little they know about what is really going on in the treatment and whether it is on or off the track. The typical treatment is no doubt off the track most of the time, yet patients somehow find a way to make the process work for them if the analyst can only learn to be patient — or, as Freud would have said, "neutral."[2] Unskilled analysts may inadvertently try to compensate for their lack of knowledge by pretending to know more than they do and behaving accordingly, an incidence of what Freud called therapeutic ambition. In Freud's view this is the most egregious example of countertransference, embodied in *inauthenticity*.

Such behavior is inauthentic because of the analyst's unwillingness *to trust the process*. What this boils down to is the analyst learning to tolerate the patient's self-disclosures by abandoning the need to over-interpret what is said. This was also a feature of Winnicott's (1989) late technique once he realized that his penchant for interpreting was actually interfering with his patients' free associations. Winnicott concluded that the principal task of psychoanalysis is to create a space where patients are free to explore their experience by speaking to it. From this angle, interpretations are not supposed to replace the patient's explanations with the analyst's, but to subvert explanations altogether. Like Freud, Winnicott concluded that the most difficult thing analysts have to learn is to dispense with demonstrating how brilliant they are, and giving their patients the time to find their own voice.

But probably the most poorly understood technical principle in Freud's nomenclature is the rule of abstinence, the technical recommendation that pertains to the patient's relationship with his or her suffering. Patients expect analysis to relieve them of suffering, but soon learn that there is a specific type of suffering they are obliged to endure in order for the therapy to be consequential. Whether we like it or not, therapy *hurts*. I don't think anyone disputes this observation in principle, though one of the most contested debates from the inception of psychoanalytic practice revolves around the question as to precisely how much it ought to hurt in order to be of value.

Freud's position on the matter was typically ambiguous, saying only, "The treatment must be carried out in abstinence ... [so that] the patient's need and longing should be allowed to persist in her, in order that they may serve as forces impelling her to do work and to make changes" (1915 [1958], p. 165). We are all familiar by now with the stereotype of the so-called classical analyst who never offers a word of encouragement or support, who sees the analytic process as a kind of deprivation chamber that is designed to inflict as much discomfort as legally permissible, and who perhaps feels giddy with the knowledge that he actually has patients who are desperate enough to allow such behavior. This type of torture, however, is not what Freud had in mind, nor was it the way he himself conducted analysis. He was conversational, engaged, alive; if anything, he was over-involved with his patients by contemporary standards.

However, Freud was not warm and cozy, compared to someone like Sandor Ferenczi. Freud saw the analytic process as an inherently painful affair that inevitably draws blood. This is because the transference revolves around a kind of expectation that one's analyst has the power to make the patient well, happy, improved, however you want to put it, instead of recognizing that the outcome of therapy always hinges on the work that *patients* accomplish, not the interventions of the analyst. The *person* of the analyst plays a role, to be sure (which I examine in Section IV, below), but not necessarily the role patients envision. The rule of abstinence speaks to whether or not analysts are in a position to help their patients in this endeavor *in the way* their patients expect them to.

What all this boils down to is that the rule of abstinence is the technical principle that Freud conceived in order to point out that it is through a kind of *disillusionment* that analysis, existential to be sure, has the power to effect change in a person's life. The term, abstinence, is perhaps unfortunate, and would be better served, I would suggest, by the *rule of authenticity*, because what we are talking about is our relationship to suffering and whether we are going to devote our lives trying to hide from it, or deciding to face it and deal with it.

III Authenticity and Suffering in the Psychoanalytic Experience

I have argued that authenticity originated in the existentialist observation that humans have a tendency to suppress their innermost being in order to relieve themselves of alienation, by abandoning their principles and abdicating their agency to forces that pull them this way or that, as long as the social incentives are compelling. I also suggested that one of the principal features of authenticity as conceived by Nietzsche, Heidegger, and Sartre is the wherewithal to *go against the grain* in one's day-to-day affairs by subjecting oneself to experiences that are undeniably painful, yet ultimately rewarding. I now want to examine how this tendency applies to the patient's efforts to avoid as much suffering as possible, and why the capacity to bear suffering is a necessary constituent of every analytic encounter. *In psychoanalysis as in existentialism, the capacity to bear suffering and the anxiety associated with being true to oneself are hallmarks of authenticity.* My thesis is that this sensibility is already latent in psychoanalysis although the term, authenticity, is seldom used to depict it.

Perhaps nowhere was Freud's authentic sensibility more aptly demonstrated than in the closing pages of his *Studies on Hysteria* (1893–1895 [1955], p. 305) where he proposed that the goal of analysis is to "transform hysterical misery into common unhappiness." One of the reasons Freud rejected happiness as a goal of therapy was the way he conceived the transference, that patients harbor fantasies about what the analyst will or should do to make them happy, or at least happier than they were. In Freud's opinion, this amounts to eliciting the analyst's love, the easy way, he says, of obtaining momentary happiness, but without having to work for it, so it cannot endure. As every analyst learns, no matter how painful this lesson turns out to be, the analyst is ultimately obliged to *thwart* such longings instead of complying with them. As noted earlier, it is through *disillusionment* that analysis effects its power to transform the neurotic from a hopeless dreamer into an individual who is willing to take life by the horns and accept its conditions, by fighting for what they want or going without it (Thompson, 2004a).

Another way of putting this is that what we *ought* to do or *should* do, when it goes against the grain of what we *desire*, manifests the split that we associate with inauthenticity. This is consistent with Freud's conception of the superego, the seat of a pseudo-morality that is fixed by introjects from one's parents and immediate environment. Essentially primitive in nature, the superego acts against our capacity for desiring by prompting us to think of what others think of us at the expense of ourselves. While this arrangement is no doubt pleasing to others, it may become a blueprint for neurotic conflicts that systematically compromise our own chances for happiness. While there are situations when we are obliged to choose an inauthentic course for non-neurotic reasons, the analyst is concerned with those choices we make that are neurotic because the choices are driven by guilt, instead of love.

Another example of authenticity in psychoanalysis is Winnicott's observation that the goal of analysis is to become a sufferer, when he linked our fear of suffering with our wish to abolish pain through omnipotence. Quoting Winnicott (1989):

> If we are successful [as analysts] we enable our patients to abandon invulnerability and [thereby] become a sufferer.

> [And], if we succeed, life will become precarious to those [patients] who were beginning to know a kind of ... freedom from pain, even if this meant non-participation in living.
>
> (p. 199)

Enigmatic though this statement sounds, Winnicott believed that *relief* from suffering was only a preliminary stage of analytic treatment that comes at a cost: non-participation in living. The real problem, as we know, is to prepare our patients for *post*-analytic existence, away from the sheltered container of the consulting room, where *life* and the anguish it occasions lead to fresh adventures that challenge us with unanticipated consequences. But why is the ability to suffer a necessary component of authenticity? This may seem like a curious question to ponder when the purported purpose of psychoanalysis is to relieve suffering, not increase it. The problem comes down to the observation that there are two kinds of suffering, not one. The first is the kind of suffering that is incumbent on everyday life and consistent with Freud's dictum that neurotics need to learn to accommodate the reality principle by delaying their gratification long enough to achieve the goals they set for themselves. The second kind of suffering is the consequence of not accommodating the first. This second, pathogenic form of suffering is peculiar to neurotic and other forms of psychopathology and is the consequence of intolerable frustration or insurmountable distress. In either case, we are left with one of three choices: 1) to look at the mess that our life has become and do something about it; 2) accept the situation we are in and live with it; or 3) or continue with the folly to which we have become adapted, and resign ourselves to it, but resentfully. Any one of these paths is painful, but it was Freud's and Winnicott's respective conclusions that the more painful path is the always the one less traveled — and the more rewarding, and therapeutic.[3]

Yet another example of authenticity in psychoanalysis is Bion's observation that, "In every consulting room there ought to be two rather frightened people; the patient and the psychoanalyst. If they are not, one wonders what they are doing there!" (1974, p. 13). Why the fear? Bion seemed to feel it has something to do with discovering something about ourselves that we would rather not know, the contrary of embracing whatever the truth about ourselves might be. One of Bion's earliest insights into the nature of the transference came when he recognized that members of the groups he led wanted to deprive him of the freedom to think what he wanted to think and to speak his mind about such thoughts accordingly. In other words, they wanted to adjudicate what he thought and what he said about them, and he recognized that one of the features of the countertransference is to succumb to this pressure by telling patients what they want to hear. Though Bion never used the term, this observation is a perfect example of how difficult it is to exercise authenticity in the analytic situation and why doing so is always uncomfortable, and often exasperating. Like Freud, in his later period Bion also advocated a prodigious use of neutrality, but whereas Freud characterized it as adopting "evenly suspended attention," Bion conceived it in terms of "erasing memory and desire" (Bion, 1967).[4] Both manners of putting it are characteristic of authenticity.

Still another example of authenticity in psychoanalysis is reflected in Lacan's famous "short session," a device he conceived as a way of thwarting the typical obsessional patient's attempts to control the analytic hour (Schneiderman, 1983, pp. 129–156). This device was consistent with Lacan's use of interpretation, which he believed should be measured in order to be optimally effective. For Lacan, the role of interpretation isn't to explain or to translate the unconscious, but to take the patient by surprise by saying something startling and thereby upsetting the patient's narcissistic relationship with the analyst. In perhaps Lacan's most explicit allusion to authenticity he advised analysts against trying to be helpful when help is asked, to abandon the wish to perform miracles, and to give up hope of terminating the treatment with the patient's gratitude for everything that has been done for them. The goal of analysis is to disappoint, and disappointment is necessarily painful and not immediately appreciated, though potentially liberating if properly digested. Though there is something undeniably Stoic about Lacan's vision of psychoanalysis, one can also recognize his debt to the existential philosophical tradition to which he was wedded in his formative years and his resistance to following the more popular analytic herd.

Yet the application of authenticity is a complicated affair and analysts may opt to emphasize some of its features in their work while neglecting it elsewhere. Freud, Winnicott, Bion, and Lacan had remarkably different, even opposing clinical styles, so the examples of their relationship with authenticity cited above shouldn't be taken to imply that the experience of being analyzed by one of them would be the same as being analyzed by another. Freud and Winnicott, for instance, permitted more of their personal relationship to intrude into their analytic space than Bion or Lacan did, who employed considerably more abstinence in their respective techniques. Yet, each of these dimensions of the treatment situation, taken in isolation, is telling of how authenticity is so relevant to the psychoanalytic process.

What all these examples share in common is the view that analysts contrive to create a situation in which analytic patients are able to finally abandon the fantasy that someone else — be it the analyst, a friend, lover, or other benefactor — will rise from the shadows to solve their problems for them, like a parent who comes to the rescue of a helpless child. No amount of reasoning or coercion will persuade us to abandon this fantasy. It is only relinquished through the nitty-gritty, day-to-day *experience* of bearing this disappointment while engaged in the work of trying to understand our resistance to it.

IV Authenticity in the Transference–Countertransference Relationship

We have discussed the philosophical and cultural underpinnings of authenticity and its roots in our relationship with suffering, how to contend with it, relieve it, and when everything fails, face it, accept it, and let it be. We also examined the elements of authentic relating in Freud's technical principles and the clinical philosophies of D. W. Winnicott, Wilfried Bion, and Jacques Lacan. I now conclude our résumé of authenticity by examining its role in the so-called transference–countertransference relationship; in fact the *extra*-transference and countertransference aspects of the analytic relationship.

There is a considered debate in the psychoanalytic literature pertaining to distinctions between so-called classical technique and more contemporary, relaxed technical standards. The prevailing view is that classical technique originated with Freud and found its culmination with American ego psychology, which is noted for an exaggerated use of abstinence and neutrality. This is confusing because classical technique, so defined, is actually foreign to the way Freud conducted psychoanalysis, as I have discussed elsewhere (1985, 1994a, 1994b, 1996a, 1996b, 1998a, 1998b, 2000a, 2000b, 2000c, 2001a, 2001b, 2002, 2004b, 2004c). Freud's conception of the transference lies at the heart of a dramatic shift in psychoanalytic technique that evolved in the post-World War II era in the New York Psychoanalytic Institute by a group of European émigrés who began to publish articles critical of the way Freud conducted his analytic treatments. In an article that shocked many of his Chicago psychoanalytic colleagues, Sam Lipton (1977) cited Freud's published treatment of the Rat Man to demonstrate the degree to which Freud's psychoanalytic behavior diverges from contemporary "classical" standards using voluminous evidence of publications by analysts — virtually all identified with ego (Freudian) psychology — who roundly condemned Freud for the technique he employed in his treatment of the Rat Man.

All the analysts cited complained about the absence of strict adherence to proper analytic principles, e.g., that Freud was too personally engaged with his patient, gave him a gift, asked to see a photo of his fiancé, fed him a meal during a therapy session, failed to consistently analyze the transference, improperly asked his patient questions, engaged in extra-interpretative, conversational dialogues with him, etc. It has been widely reported by Freud's former patients how personally engaging he was as an analyst, that some even complained that he talked too much, that he invited some to accompany him on vacations, that he spoke openly of his personal problems with patients he was fond of, and so on. Freud did not report these "interventions" in his case reports[5] because he did not view them as *technical* interventions; they were part of his ongoing personal relationship with patients that he believed were not worth noting. The criticisms are surprising on two counts. First, because Freud's treatment of the Rat Man was successful and was used as a teaching tool in virtually every psychoanalytic institute in the world until Freud's death. It was only in the late 1940s that his analytic technique was deemed inadequate by so-called classical standards. Second, these criticisms suggest that the definition of classical technique changed after Freud's death into what is now defined as the standard for classical technique, yet this technique is erroneously attributed to Freud by more *contemporary* (non-Freudian) analysts who condemn this technique for its excessive use of detachment in the therapy relationship. What accounts for this shift in technique, as envisioned by so-called Freudian analysts? I believe that the most telling feature of *revised* classical technique is its reconceptualization of the transference by omitting from the analyst–analysand relationship all vestiges of the personal, or real, relationship. Moreover, I propose that the effort to "protect" the analyst from the personal elements of the relationship shared with patients serves as a source of inauthenticity and robs the relationship of genuineness, which patients hope to experience and invariably complain about if it is absent.

The situation is so confusing that Lipton proposed that this *newer*, post-World War II technique that evolved during the late 1940s and early 1950s should be termed "modern" instead of classical in order to distinguish it from Freud's which, because it came earlier, should be termed classical. This is not likely to happen, so we are left with the unfortunate dilemma of *two* classical techniques, one belonging to Freud and the other belonging to ego psychology but claiming to originate with Freud, though ego psychologists complain that Freud himself did not practice it! (Thompson, 1994a, pp. 230–240).

American ego psychology identifies itself with Freud and claims to be adhering to technical principles that he advocated, but did not follow. The principal objection they raised concerns the way they perceived the interplay between Freud's *personal* relationship with the Rat Man and Freud's narrow *technical* interventions. Some analysts saw Freud's personal relationship with the Rat Man — e.g., feeding him a meal when he had apparently not eaten for days — as a *technical intervention* designed to manipulate the transference, but claim that Freud did not satisfactorily deal with this unconventional "intervention" and that, in hindsight, he should have refrained from doing so. It seems that none of these analysts were able to fathom what Freud had in mind with any of the personal asides he engaged in *unless* they were intended as expressions of technique; in other words, it was impossible to conceive his behavior as specifically personal in nature. Lipton concludes that, "The essence of the difference between modern/classical technique and Freud's is that the definition of [this newer] technique has been expanded to incorporate aspects of the analyst's relation with the patient which Freud excluded from technique" (p. 262). In other words, Freud recognized both a personal relationship as well as a transference relationship that co-existed side by side during the course of a patient's treatment. The personal relationship was not typically subjected to analysis or interpretation unless there was a compelling reason for doing so.

In order to appreciate this distinction and why ego psychologists had difficulty understanding Freud's clinical behavior, I will briefly review the way Freud conceived the nature of the transference and how this technical principle has evolved since his death. The concept of transference, which Freud invented, has become so confusing that *non*-psychoanalytic existential therapists have summarily excluded it from their conception of the therapeutic process! For Freud, transference was essentially another word for love and ubiquitous to the human experience. It goes on everywhere, in and outside the analytic relationship, so the only thing that is special about the emergence of the transference (the patient's love for the analyst) in analysis is that instead of acting on such feelings they are examined and talked about, *without* acting on them. Freud distinguished among three kinds of transference: positive and negative; and the positive transference was divided again into two, the erotic and unobjectionable. Both negative and erotic components of the transference are unconscious and serve as sources of resistance, whereas the unobjectionable transference comprises conscious feelings of affection or positive regard toward the analyst and the work they are engaged in collaboratively. Remember that for Freud analysis is about the *work* accomplished and suffered. The transference can either further this process or engender a wish that the analyst will cure the patient's ills through magic or infantile, idealized editions of love, manifesting incidents of resistance that should be pointed out to one's patient and discussed.

Now love has a role, but a subtle one. To equate transference with love is a complicated claim and demands a concerted exploration into its nature, both its mature and regressive editions. Unlike most contemporary classical analysts, Freud believed that love plays a critical role in the outcome of every analysis. Why, after all, would anyone put up with all the anguish and heartache that the work of analysis demands from patients if it weren't for the bond of affection felt for the analyst by the typical patient? Freud was aware that this kind of positive (unobjectionable) transference was crucial for a desirable outcome for the therapy, not because love heals, but because without it who would be willing to stay the course through all the difficulty expected of them? Separating this form of love from the infantile projections that urge the analyst to abandon all vestiges of abstinence is not easy, but Freud expected that every analyst should be equipped to perform this role with sufficient preparation and training. One form of love Freud deemed personal, whereas the other he conceived as a technical component of the transference (Freud, 1915 [1958]).

Perhaps in order to make matters appear less ambiguous, Kanzer (1952) and Kris (1951) were in the vanguard of analysts who expanded the concept of transference to include the entirety of the patient's relationship with the analyst, so the idea of a personal — or what Freud termed unobjectionable — dimension to the analyst–patient interaction became moot. Until this development it was common for analysts to engage in conversations with their patients and to make non-analytic comments of a personal nature, ask questions, even disclose information about themselves, and so on.[6] Now analysts were expected to speak only when giving interpretations but to otherwise remain silent. Why did this happen? Lipton suspects this developed by accident when Eissler (1953), in a paper condemning Franz Alexander's expansion of transference to include personal gestures by the analyst, advocated a revision of technique that encouraged a *minimum* of analytic interventions, apart from the use of interpretations. This paper had a decisive impact on the analytic community, partly because New York analysts were searching for a way to marginalize what they saw as Alexander's corruption of proper analytic technique.

In short order all the other elements that we have come to associate with classical technique coalesced into its current form: 1) a concerted attention to the analyst's behavior instead of his purpose; 2) the exclusion of the analyst's *personality* from the treatment; 3) the use of the analyst's silence as a mode of communication instead of a mode of listening. Ironically, efforts to eliminate the personal relationship from the analytic discourse are not only ill advised, but also patently impossible. Moreover, such attention to detail has the effect of placing too much weight on minor matters instead of major ones, and lends to classical technique a prospective or prophylactic approach instead of a retrospective one. Instead of occupying himself with examining the meaning of his patient's associations, the analyst diverts a great deal of his attention to excluding interventions that would otherwise become the subject of future associations and discussion. This diverts the analyst's attentiveness from a neutral state of mind to a critical one. And what does the potential impact that working in this fashion have on the personality of a typical classical analyst? She is more liable to become shy, cautions, tentative, circumspect, and inhibited in her demeanor instead of bold, creative, adventurous, self-confident, and spontaneous. Even the selection process of potential analytic candidates in training institutes is more likely to favor obsessional types over hysterics, as history has demonstrated.

Presumably most "modern" classical analysts have recognized the impossible situation they put themselves in after removing the personal relationship because they were subsequently obliged to reinsert it in the guise of the so-called therapeutic alliance, which now becomes, not strictly personal in the conventional sense but a part of the technical, analytic relationship, because it is subject to analysis and interpretation. Obviously there is a difference between a dimension of a relationship that I have with a person that occurs naturally and spontaneously and one that I know is laden with hidden meanings and unconscious intentions: one that my analyst will always, after the fact, inform me about as to what I was really thinking of or up to when such and such was said or shared between us. Lipton even suggests that utilizing a working alliance can be injurious to the analytic relationship:

> Devoting explicit attention to [the working alliance] encumbers the analysis with a series of dangers and disadvantages. It tends to foster artificiality; tends to give undue weight to the analyst's behavior; tends to expand technique beyond the area which the patient knows about and collaborates with; and tends to substitute for the genuine, personal relationship on which the analysis is based, an idealized relationship in which the patient meets not another person but a sort of encompassing, technically-correct instrumentality.
>
> (1977, p. 266)

In effect, all vestiges of the personal relationship shared with patients have been transformed into aspects of the patient's transference with the analyst, which the analyst is obliged to interpret accordingly. From the classical perspective, transference has become a rarefied, trance-like state of childlike hypnotic regression that places the patient in a one-down position from which she cannot easily extricate herself, because she is always "in" the transference, which she cannot get out of. This has the chilling effect of perceiving the analysand as never really being the author of his or her experience or a proper adult in an I–Thou relationship, but the "effect" of unconscious forces that only the analyst is privy to. In other words, the concept of transference has become a vehicle of *defense* against the realness of the person of the patient in treatment, whenever it is convenient for the analyst to remove himself from the impact of proximity with his patients. So instead of using the transference/countertransference situation as a means of obtaining intimacy, of moving back and forth between the specific work of the treatment and the relationship shared between them, the so-called classical analyst rejects any vestige of extra-analytic engagement and interprets any incidence of closeness or informality as seduction, or "transference."

So what are the criteria of the personal relationship that so many analysts find so frightening that they have been factored out of the treatment? Unlike technical aspects of the treatment situation, there cannot be universal standards for how a given analyst is going to use his or her person in the treatment with each patient. Freud wasn't even comfortable with mandating strict standards for the application of his technical principles, let alone the personal ones! As a rule of thumb, however, what is deemed personal should be obvious. It is both outside technique and subject to individual variation. It cannot be codified because, just as analysts differ from person to person, each analyst's conception of the personal relationship will vary as well. Moreover, analysts are liable to form different conceptions of what the personal relationship entails at different stages of their careers and with different patients, when they inhabit different moods, and so on. Even narrow interpretations need clarification and expansion and such conversational digressions require a departure from strict interpretative speech. The many times that analysts must talk to their patients about such matters as whether the analysis is working for them, whether they should use the couch, disagreements as to matters of frequency, absence from sessions, increase in fees, and so on, have to be hammered out on a person to person basis that ultimately comes down to how credible the analyst is in the eyes of their patient. In my experience of these situations, the concept of a therapeutic alliance has been of little help in ironing these issues out.

For the personal relationship to be spontaneous, unpredictable, and authentic it has to be free of contrivance and guile. Yet sometimes it isn't so easy to tell when it is personal and when it is transference. Otto Will, the student of Harry Stack Sullivan and Frieda Fromm-Reichmann and former Director of Chestnut Lodge Hospital and Austen Riggs Center, once told me a story of his analysis with Sullivan that may serve as an apt example. This was an uncomfortable period in his analysis and Will was feeling frustrated with the progress of his treatment and with Sullivan, who could be difficult under the best of circumstances. Finally, one day Will blurted out that he felt angry with Sullivan. Will immediately felt guilty for his outburst and said in so many words that he was sorry for his behavior and supposed that this was evidence of his father transference emerging. Sullivan immediately corrected Will and said, "No, Doctor, that was not your father transference. It just so happens that right now you don't like me very much and I don't like you, but I'm sure if we persevere we'll get through it somehow" (Will, personal communication, 1992). The distinction may seem arbitrary, but it is typical of the way Freud, Fenichel, Glover, Winnicott, and a legion of other analysts have typically distinguished between personal and transference communications between their patients and themselves, the one suggesting interpretation, the other a simple acknowledgment of feelings that *analyst and patient happen to be feeling for each other.*

The most common incidence of the personal relationship that exists in the analytic relationship is ultimately embodied in the forms of *conversation* that evolve between them. Classical analysts tend to reject the term because they argue that "conversing" has no discernable role in the analytic discourse. The patient speaks and the analyst interprets; conversation, as such, is avoided. Yet Freud conversed freely with his patients and engaged in straightforward dialogues with them, a form of speech that has subsequently become *verboten* to classical analysts (Racker, 1968, p. 35). This form of conversation is obviously gratifying for patient and analyst alike and is necessarily restrained by the rule of abstinence, but to abandon it entirely is artificial. It serves as an exemplary tool for furthering free association when employed skillfully, but it is also a humanizing aspect of the analyst's personal relationship with each patient, showing concern for each patient as a person with whom he or she is engaged, helping to prolong the treatment toward an optimal conclusion. Analysts reveal personal things about themselves to patients mature enough to contain them, and when patients make personal observations about their analysts they are not always interpreted as projections, but sometimes astute observations that may be taken as compliments or criticisms. Naturally, one monitors what occurs in such conversations and brings their content under scrutiny *when appropriate*, but not necessarily or systematically as when addressing components of a technical regimen. Permitting one's personality to become part of the constellation of elements that patients experience serves as an invaluable source for authentic relating and complements the exercise of technical principles discussed earlier. It is this personal dimension to the relationship between therapist and patients that is the nodal point of *existential psychoanalysis*.

But probably the principal motive for engaging in a personal relationship with patients is that there is no good reason not to, because this is the context in which the patient experiences genuine love for the analyst, not love as a projection or idealization or regression to infantile fixations, but the genuine and real edition of love that manifests itself in the course of just about every analysis, and without which a meaningful analysis is impossible to imagine. How could patients be expected to put up with the trials and tribulations they are subjected to during the course of their treatment if not for the love they come to develop for their analyst in the first place? It is relevant that few analysts talk about love or acknowledge its relevance to the analytic process, and most analysts go out of their way to insist that it has no role to speak of. Indeed, the concept of transference, once synonymous with love, is now viewed as little more than an algebraic equation, a place on the map occupied by one participant acting out a fantasy onto a blank screen whose function is little more than to interpret back as accurately as possible the etchings of the projections recorded. Anything of a personal nature is checked at the door and retrieved at the termination of treatment, if then.

In short, the capacity to acknowledge the existence of a personal relationship with patients, to accept and freely engage it in a manner of one's choosing and that complements their need for intimacy, lends a dimension of genuineness to the relationship that has profound implications for the way therapy is experienced, and even how the technical principles are construed. Intuitively, most analysts know this and conduct themselves accordingly. Recent controversies in analytic technique under the rubric of relational and contemporary perspectives have targeted these very issues, though some of the authors fail to recognize that the so-called classical technique they rightfully condemn has little relation to Freud's treatment philosophy or behavior, but is the creature of a more recent lineage. As I shall point out in the next chapter, even relational psychoanalysts, who claim to be less austere than the aforementioned classical analysts, employ circumscribed techniques of their own.

V Conclusion

In conclusion, what do the foregoing clinical examples of authenticity share in common with the way the concept was conceived by Nietzsche, Heidegger, and Sartre? Although Freud, Winnicott, Bion, and Lacan never invoked the term as a feature of their analytic technique, the way each rejects the easier and undoubtedly more comforting strategy of doing everything one can to please one's patients in the hope this will elicit an easier treatment experience is a critical feature of how Nietzsche and Heidegger in particular characterized authentic being in the world. On the other hand, we have also seen how easily analysts just as frequently take the opposite tack in *doing nothing* to reach out to their patients, and talk to them, but hold them at arm's length in order to mitigate the anxiety they feel for being at close quarters to another human being. The treatment is obviously not served by this. This isn't a moral position, but a recognition that change is necessarily painful and requires sacrifice, so if analysts expect their patients to shoulder the quota of sacrifices they need to in order to benefit from the treatment, then the analyst has to be willing and able to shoulder the same measure of sacrifice him or herself.

What this comes down to is that the analyst instills the capacity for sacrifice in his patients *through his own example*. This instilling is not a matter of technique that can simply be "applied" from the comfort of detaching oneself from the process, but an *act of courage* that has to be suffered, repeatedly and constantly throughout the treatment with each patient. This is why the wherewithal to endure the first kind of suffering discussed earlier in order to mitigate the second kind is what Freud, Winnicott, Bion, and Lacan had in mind when they concluded that, not only life but analysis entails suffering. Though none of them used the term, the wisdom of submitting to suffering and making use of it makes little sense without at least an instinctive awareness of the role that authenticity properly plays in all of our clinical endeavors, whether we call ourselves existentialists or not.

Notes

1 See Charles Taylor, 1991, for a conception of authenticity that embraces a moral perspective.
2 Actually, *indifferent* in the original German.
3 For the relation between Winnicott's thesis of a true-self and false-self system and authenticity see Jon Mills, 2003 and R. D. Laing, 1960.
4 *Erasing memory* for Bion refers to staying in the present and treating each session as though it was the first. *Erasing desire* is Bion's term for avoiding therapeutic ambition, by suspending judgment as to what one expects or hopes to happen from the analytic experience, and to simply let things be and see where they go: neutrality in its essence.
5 The gist of these extra-analytic interventions was revealed in case notes that Freud typically destroyed after he published his cases, but for some reason were left intact in the case of the *Rat Man*. Strachey included them in his translation of Freud's case report of the *Standard Edition*.
6 I am describing the way analysts who were identified with the classical approach of Freud tended to work. Analysts such as Melanie Klein developed a more austere form of analytic technique that dispensed with personal engagement with patients by employing abstinence to unprecedented degrees. In this regard Klein is even more austere than ego psychologists!

References

Binswanger, L. (1963) *Being-in-the-world: Selected papers of Ludwig Binswanger* (J. Needleman, trans.). New York: Basic Books.
Bion, W. R. (1967) Notes on memory and desire. *Psychoanalytic Forum*, Volume 2: 271–280.
Bion, W. R. (1974) *Bion's Brazilian lectures—1*. Rio de Janeiro: Imago Editora Ltda.
Boss, M. (1963) *Psychoanalysis and daseinsanalysis*. L. Lefebre, trans.). New York and London: Basic Books.
Breuer, J. and Freud, S. (1893–1895 [1955]) *Studies on hysteria. Standard edition*, 2: 1–305. London: Hogarth Press.
Eissler, K. R. (1953) The effect of the structure of the ego on psychoanalytic technique. *Journal of the American Psychoanalytic Association*, Volume 1: 104–143.
Freud, S. (1915 [1958]) Observations on transference-love (Further *recommendations* on the technique of psycho-analysis III). *Standard edition*, 12: 157–171. London: Hogarth Press.
Freud, S. (1930 [1961]) *Civilization and its discontents. Standard edition*, 21: 59–145. London: The Hogarth Press.

Groarke, L. (1990) *Greek scepticism: Anti-realist trends in ancient thought.* Montreal and London: McGill-Queen's University Press.

Heidegger, M. (1962) *Being and time* (J. Macquarrie and E. Robinson, trans.). New York: Harper and Row.

Kanzer, M. (1952) The transference neurosis of the Rat Man. *The Psychoanalytic Quarterly*, Volume 21: 181–189.

Kris, E. (1951) Ego psychology and interpretation in psychoanalytic therapy. *The Psychoanalytic Quarterly*, Volume 20: 15–30.

Laing, R. D. (1960) *The divided self.* New York: Pantheon Books.

Laing, R. D. (1969) *Self and others* (2nd rev. ed.). New York: Pantheon Books.

Leavy, S. (1980) *The psychoanalytic dialogue.* New Haven, CT and London: Yale University Press.

Leavy, S. (1988) *In the image of God: A psychoanalyst's view.* New Haven, CT and London: Yale University Press.

Lipton, S. (1977) The advantages of Freud's technique as shown in his analysis of the rat man. *The International Journal of Psychoanalysis*, Volume 58: 255–273.

Loewald, H. W. (1980) *Papers on psychoanalysis.* New Haven, CT and London: Yale University Press.

Mills, J. (2003) A phenomenology of becoming: Reflections on authenticity. In R. Frie (Ed.), *Understanding experience: Psychotherapy and postmodernism*, pp. 137–160. London and New York: Routledge.

Mitchell, S. A. (1992) True selves, false selves, and the ambiguity of authenticity. In N. J. Skolnick and S. C. Warshaw (Eds.), *Relational perspectives in psychoanalysis.* Hillsdale, NJ: Analytic Press.

Nietzsche, F. (2002) *Beyond good and evil* (J. Norman, trans.). Cambridge: Cambridge University Press.

Nietzsche, F. (2003) *Writing from the late notebooks* (K. Sturge, trans.). Cambridge: Cambridge University Press.

Racker, H. (1968) *Transference and countertransference.* New York: International Universities Press.

Schneiderman, S. (1983) *Jacques Lacan: The death of an intellectual hero.* Cambridge, MA and London: Harvard University Press.

Taylor, C. (1991) *The ethics of authenticity.* Cambridge, MA and London: Harvard University Press.

Thompson, M. G. (1985) *The death of desire: A study in psychopathology.* New York and London: New York University Press.

Thompson, M. G. (1994a) *The truth about Freud's technique: The encounter with the real.* New York and London: New York University Press.

Thompson, M. G. (1994b) The existential dimension to termination. *Psychoanalysis and Contemporary Thought*, Volume 17, No. 3: 355–386.
Thompson, M. G. (1996a) The rule of neutrality. *Psychoanalysis and Contemporary Thought*, Volume 19, No. 1: 57–84.
Thompson, M. G. (1996b) Freud's conception of neutrality. *Contemporary Psychoanalysis*, Volume 32, No. 1: 25–42.
Thompson, M. G. (1998a) Manifestations of transference: Love, friendship, rapport. *Contemporary Psychoanalysis*, Volume 34, No. 4: 543–561.
Thompson, M. G. (1998b) The fundamental rule of psychoanalysis. *The Psychoanalytic Review*, Volume 85, No. 5: 697–715.
Thompson, M. G. (2000a) The sceptic dimension of psychoanalysis: Toward an ethic of experience. *Contemporary Psychoanalysis*, Volume 36, No. 3: 457–481.
Thompson, M. G. (2000b) The crisis of experience in contemporary psychoanalysis. *Contemporary Psychoanalysis*, Volume 36, No. 1: 29–56.
Thompson, M. G. (2000c) Scepticism and psychoanalysis. *Psychologist-Psychoanalyst*, Volume 20, No. 2..
Thompson, M. G. (2001a) The ethic of psychoanalysis: The fundamental rule to be honest. In A. Molino (Ed.), *Where Id was: Challenging normalization in psychoanalysis*, pp. 73–86. London: Athlone Press.
Thompson, M. G. (2001b) The enigma of honesty: The fundamental rule of psychoanalysis. *Free Associations*, Volume 8, No. 47: 390–434.
Thompson, M. G. (2001c) Is the unconscious really all that unconscious? The role of being and experience in the psychoanalytic encounter. *Contemporary Psychoanalysis*, Volume 37, No. 4: 571–612.
Thompson, M. G. (2002) The existential dimension to working through. *Journal of the Society for Existential Analysis*, Volume 13, No. 1..
Thompson, M. G. (2004a) Happiness and chance: A reappraisal of the psychoanalytic conception of suffering. *Psychoanalytic Psychology*. Volume 21, No. 1: 134–153.
Thompson, M. G. (2004b) *The ethic of honesty: The fundamental rule of psychoanalysis*. Amsterdam and New York: Editions Rodopi.
Thompson, M. G. (2004c) Postmodernism and psychoanalysis: A Heideggerian critique of postmodern malaise and the question of authenticity. In J. Reppen, M. Schulman, and J. Tucker (Eds.), *Way beyond Freud: Postmodern psychoanalysis evaluated*. London: Open Gate Press.

Thompson, M. G. (2004d) Nietzsche and psychoanalysis: The fate of authenticity in a postmodernist world. *Journal of the Society for Existential Analysis*, Volume 15, No. 2..

Winnicott, D. W. (1989) *Psychoanalytic explorations* (C. Winnicott, R. Shephard, and M. David, Eds.). Cambridge, MA: Harvard University Press.

Zahavi, D. (2001) *Husserl and transcendental subjectivity.* Athens, OH: Ohio University Press.

Chapter 4

The Demise of the Person in Psychoanalysis

The Deconstruction of the Personal Relationship

The heart and soul of existential psychoanalysis is the *personal dimension* to the relationship between therapist and patient. This is sorely missing in the psychoanalytic literature, and even relational psychoanalysis, which purports to correct this problem, is nonetheless plagued with technical interventions that place severe limits on any hint of a personal relationship between the two protagonists. As I will endeavor to show in this, the final chapter of this book, even existential *therapists*, who advocate a person-based approach to psychotherapy, remain surprisingly wedded to techniques that they claim are alien to a specifically psychoanalytic frame of reference. In this concluding essay I will articulate what sets existential psychoanalysis apart from other schools of psychoanalysis, as well as other schools of existential therapy, counseling, and the like.

First, I want to say that there is nothing "wrong" with existential therapy that is explicitly or implicitly opposed to psychoanalysis. Nor do I feel that there is anything wrong with a psychoanalysis that is not in any form or fashion indebted to or conversant with existential philosophy. I feel that all schools of psychotherapy, psychoanalytic, existential, humanistic, cognitive behavioral, and so on, have their value, and that they help people who need someone to talk to about their problems, and their life. I don't need to put down or dismiss other schools of therapy in order to advocate the efficacy of an integration of existential

DOI: 10.4324/9781003595427-4

philosophy and psychoanalysis. This union, or integration, enjoys its own merits, just as all the other types of therapy enjoy theirs. So what is it that is distinctive about existential psychoanalysis, the way that I see it, and practice it?

I think that the best way of articulating this distinction is by examining the role of the *person* in existential psychoanalysis, and the features that I believe make existential psychoanalysis the most person-based form of psychotherapy. In order to accomplish this I will have to take us on a journey into the way that psychoanalysis was originally conceived by Freud, the role that he assigned to the personal dimension of the relationship between analyst and patient, and especially the role of the person in his theories about the unconscious and transference phenomena, the cardinal elements of how we customarily, to this day, define "psychoanalysis." The title of this chapter, *The Demise of the Person in Psychoanalysis*, alludes to alleged non-personal elements in psychoanalysis, and I hope to use this chapter to highlight what I think makes existential psychoanalysis distinctive.

I readily admit that the notion of a "demise of the person" in the psychoanalytic process may seem like a strange choice of subject matter for a concluding chapter. After all, the words person and personal are not even technical terms in standard psychoanalytic nomenclature. Both words are typically invoked, if at all, in a strictly offhand way when referring to non-transferential and non-technical behavior and experience in the context of the psychoanalytic treatment relationship. For the majority of analysts so-called personal aspects of the treatment situation have little if any role to play in the psychoanalytic process as it is typically conceived. For many, it is the absence of a personal engagement with patients that distinguishes psychoanalysis from its more user-friendly cousins, psychodynamic psychotherapy, existential therapies, and so on. Psychodynamic psychotherapy is admittedly distinguished from *psychoanalysis* proper by its relatively relaxed technique. This usually implies that their patients are not using the couch, but meet face to face, and that the frequency of sessions may be as infrequent as weekly or twice weekly. Analysts typically insist that four times a week is optimal, and even necessary to qualify as a genuine psychoanalysis, though three times a week has now been rendered acceptable by the International Psychoanalytical Association, the governing body founded by Freud. Yet, "psychoanalytic therapist" may simply pertain to someone who has not graduated from a psychoanalytic institute, and should therefore not claim to be a *psychoanalyst*. Moreover, therapists who call themselves "psychodynamic" may be just as rigid about the definition of boundaries as *bona fide* psychoanalysts are!

It has become increasingly commonplace that contemporary psychoanalysts of virtually all persuasions reduce the psychoanalytic process to the analysis of transference, resistance, and more recently — a term introduced by relational psychoanalysts — enactments. This has resulted in the general assumption that virtually *all* of a patient's reactions to the person of the analyst should be treated as transference manifestations. Similarly, most if not all significant interventions by the analyst in response to transference phenomena are invariably informed by whichever technical principles a given analyst elects to follow. This is a view typically held, for example, by Kleinian, classical Freudian (i.e. American ego psychology), and most contemporary relational analysts, all of whom tend to deconstruct the very notion of a person-to-person engagement out of the psychoanalytic process. Such analysts often concede that interactions of a personal nature invariably occur during every therapeutic encounter, but such occurrences are usually deemed irrelevant and even impediments to the analytic process and are scrupulously avoided or, when unavoidable, systematically analyzed.

As a topical example of just how far this attitude has evolved, I cite an article in *Psychoanalytic Psychology* (Maroda, 2007), which was subsequently discussed in the *New York Times*, that questioned the efficacy of analysts treating patients in their home office. The author of the article, Karen Maroda, offered that such arrangements may serve as "keyholes" into the analyst's personal life and consequently "over stimulate and overwhelm" patients. She argues that any contact with the analyst's personal life will inevitably result in an unsettling, even harmful experience (if indeed knowledge of a personal nature about one's analyst is inherently traumatic).

Even a cursory survey of the psychoanalytic literature over the course of its long history shows how surprisingly recent the trend to "depersonalize" the psychoanalytic relationship in fact is. Unfortunately, this bias is increasingly followed by mental health practitioners generally, as a rule of thumb. An extraordinary number of seminal contributors to matters of technique — including Sigmund Freud, Sandor Ferenczi, Theodor Reik, Ronald Fairbairn, D. W. Winnicott, Peter Lomas, Erik Erikson, Hans Loewald, Leo Stone, Erich Fromm, Stan Leavy, Sam Lipton, R. D. Laing, and many others — believe on the contrary that the personal relationship between patient and analyst should be acknowledged in order to accommodate the unpredictable nature of the *total* psychotherapeutic encounter. These analysts argue that a wide assortment of object relations, in addition to transference phenomena, occur over the course of every psychoanalytic treatment, and that the astute handling of such non-transference and non-technical interactions are an indispensable component of the therapeutic process. On the other hand Ferenczi, an important advocate of informal technique, may inadvertently serve as a confusing model for a more personally engaged way of conducting psychoanalytic and other psychotherapeutic treatments. For example, Ferenczi was noted for his gregarious and affectionate personality in the way he typically behaved with his patients. Ferenczi also engaged in a series of *technical* experiments that were designed to make the psychoanalytic process more democratic and less authoritarian. Ferenczi is often cited by contemporary relational analysts (Davies and Frawley, 1991; Ogden, 1994; Mitchell and Black, 1995) as the first advocate of a two-person psychology, yet his inherently outgoing personality traits are typically confused with his more deliberate technical innovations, so that both are erroneously conceived as aspects of *technique*, in the strict sense of that term. Consequently, the specifically spontaneous, unpredictable attributes of a given psychoanalyst's personality have been incorporated into deliberate, circumscribed technical recommendations that effectively compromise the uniquely personal component of the analyst's participation in the process.

Another example of this development can be found among relational analysts who take umbrage with the more classical characterization of transference phenomena as *distortions* of the patient's real or realistic perception of the analyst's behavior. Relational analysts argue — in my opinion, correctly — that such perceptions *may* (or may not) be accurate and even insightful observations of the analyst's behavior, about which the analyst may be unaware. Yet, in so doing, these same relational analysts tend to treat such ostensibly accurate perceptions as aspects of the patient's transference. Consequently, such perceptions are not conceived as components of the ongoing *personal* relationship, but rather as an "expanded" notion of how classical analysts typically conceive the transference situation. For instance, whereas Hoffman (1983) advocates more spontaneity and truthfulness in the analytic relationship, his principal concern is a technical matter, that analysts should encourage their patients to reflect upon and verbalize how they are experiencing their relationship with their analyst. Hoffman points out that analysts have traditionally not been taught to perform such interventions. Moreover, he believes that many of the analysts (e.g., Leo Stone, Hans Loewald, James Strachey, Ralph Greenson, Robert Langs, Heinz Kohut) who have emphasized the importance of the real or personal relationship existing alongside the transferential do not encourage their patients to verbalize their experiences about their relationship. He also chides these analysts for adhering to the traditional depiction of transference phenomena as "distortions" of what is really occurring in the analyst–analysand dynamic, thereby setting themselves up as authorities on what is real and what is not. Analysts who encourage more personal or human engagement with their patients fall prey to what Hoffman sees as a stubborn adherence to the analyst as authority figure to the patient as supplicant; these analysts may be compassionate, but they call the shots as to what is actually going on. This characterization of so-called classical or orthodox analysts has been roundly criticized by Haynal (1997) for oversimplifying the complexity of the historical evolution of psychoanalytic theory and technique over the past century, especially in Europe.

I admit to being puzzled by Hoffman's criticisms. It would seem to me that a relational perspective that is firmly rooted in the Interpersonal tradition (initiated by Sullivan and subsequently developed by Fromm, Fromm-Reichmann, C. Thompson, O. Will, and numerous others) would privilege spontaneity *and* personal engagement by both analyst and analysand, a manner of engagement that cannot be reduced to technical interventions, however enlightened or perceptive such interventions may be. Hoffman complains that there is no way of distinguishing between personal and transferential aspects of the analytic dyad and claims that even Freud, with his conception of the unobjectionable transference,[1] observed that transference is ubiquitous in virtually all human relationships. Hoffman chastises Stone, for example, for claiming that the transferential and real relationships are distinct but intertwined when he says that "the transference will, under [certain] circumstances, include realistic perceptions of the analyst" (1983, p. 49). Hoffman argues that Stone cannot have it both ways, to say that one can distinguish between the two and yet insist they can commingle.

It seems to me that Hoffman is genuinely confused about the distinction between the personal and technical aspects of the analytic experience and, so, reduces it to unrelenting tech-ridden interventions that pervade the treatment situation. This problem probably originates with how Freud envisioned matters of technique and the subtle differences between real and transferential love, outlined in Freud's seminal and most exhaustive paper on the nature of love, "Observations on Transference-Love" (1915 [1958]). Because Freud saw transference phenomena as contemporary editions of the patient's Oedipal, unrequited love, he recognized that so-called transference experiences occur in all human encounters, including outside the analytic situation. We only call this phenomenon *transference* (instead of love) in the context of analysis because no one can fall in love with their analyst as innocently as they might otherwise in the normal course of events. This is because the comportment of the analyst with whom the patient forms a positive transference is essentially a *contrivance*. The analyst does not show concern, curiosity, and compassion for the patient because of the compelling character traits the analysand happens to possess. He does so because that is what he is being paid to do; it is his job. That doesn't, however, mean that the feelings of concern and compassion he displays toward his patient are not genuine. They are. They are two human beings who spend a lot of time together and the analyst feels these things because that is what makes him or her human. He may also harbor his own personal reasons for wanting to help people. Perhaps he took care of his mother when he was a child and developed a tolerance for such uncommonly intimate and intense relationships that he has (unconsciously) opted to turn this talent into a vocation. The patient is effectively thrown into an intensive relationship not unlike she might with a married colleague. Familiarity breeds intimacy and the situation that brings people together may elicit emotional reactions that they would otherwise never experience with that person. Usually this happens by accident. In psychoanalysis it is deliberate.

Another way of putting it is that transference is ubiquitous because our capacity for love is universal and always operative. If we were not capable of such feelings we would not be effective practitioners. Indeed, it is a prerequisite for and the foundation of every intimate relationship we have. The personal and the transferential do blend, but they can readily be distinguished, with some effort and attentiveness. A patient may come to trust me because I remind him of his grandfather whom he loved and admired, but also because I treat him in such a way that warrants such trust. The technique of non-judgmental neutrality is not just a "technique": it speaks to my capacity to suspend judgment and keep an open mind, a personal attribute that some people possess more of than others. When this furthers my patient's analytic attitude and his or her ability to free associate and reflect on my interpretations I don't necessarily have to bring it to my patient's attention that "this is only transference, you know," even if that is the case. It is a judgment call as to when and how often I feel the need to offer explicit transference interpretations, be they of the genetic, transferential, or here-and-now variety.[2] But the technique of rendering such interventions occurs in the context of a personal relationship that is guided by our respective character traits, including our respective capacities for intimacy, candor, and affiliation. Hoffman seems so intent on bringing our attention to a favored technique that he ends up throwing out the baby of personal engagement with the bathwater of classical technique.

Hoffman advocates a less dogmatic and more skeptical manner of sharing interpretations with his patients, and I applaud him for that. Behaving more compassionately and sensitively with one's patients is a no-brainer. But in my view, the inherently personal aspects of the analyst–patient relationship should not necessarily be subject to analysis nor should they always fall under the rubric of technique. That which is personal is, by its nature, generally taken for granted and permitted to pass as that dimension of the analytic relationship that is both genuine and authentic. *It is from this foundation of the ongoing personal relationship that transference phenomena derive.* Indeed, the recognition of the ubiquitous nature of the personal relationship between analyst and patient and its development are the hallmarks of a genuinely *existential* conception of psychoanalysis. The significance of the distinction between the personal and the technical aspects of existential psychoanalysis will become more apparent below.

What accounts for this glaring dichotomy in our conception of the personal relationship and why is there such reluctance to recognize and, in turn, systematically explore the vital role this relationship plays in the analytic process? Why does the word "personal" arouse so much concern that it has been more or less banished from our characterization of the process, and relegated to psychoanalytic "psychotherapy"? Finally, what role does the psychoanalytic conception of the unconscious play in these considerations, and how did our conception of transference as a strictly unconscious phenomenon become incompatible with the notion of a personal dimension to the analytic relationship?

It is a common assumption that the unconscious is the pivot around which psychoanalytic theory and practice orbit and distinguishes psychoanalysis from other kinds of psychotherapy, such as CBT, family therapy, humanistic, psychodynamic, and even existential therapies that are hostile to psychoanalysis. It necessarily follows that one of the cardinal questions raised by the psychoanalytic conception of the unconscious is the role of the subject or person who is engaged in this therapeutic endeavor.

Freud's earlier topographical model addressed this question ambiguously when he coined the term, *Gegenwille* ("counter-will" in English) in order to locate the role of unconscious motivation and how intentions can be operative yet unknown to the person (Leavy, 1988). The term *will* has been historically marginalized by psychoanalysts for a variety of reasons. Being a verb as well as a noun, the term always implies a subject. When I do something that I claim I didn't mean or intend to, it does no good to plead that blind, impersonal forces "did" the act. Those so-called unconscious forces are *me*.

Counter-will served as an early marker for how Freud conceived the unconscious as a subject who *performs acts* about which the actor is to varying degrees unaware. Though this term endured for some twenty years, after 1912 it more or less disappeared as the generalization collapsed into concepts like resistance, repression, unconscious conflict, and drive. Freud's subsequent structural model cemented this process even further, when he explicitly depersonalized unconscious agency in the language of id, superego, and defense mechanisms. But the gain in specificity was accompanied by the loss of a *personal*, as well as responsible, will. As Freud pursued his project of establishing the empirical causes of symptoms, his earlier notion of the unconscious as a secret agent or anonymous ego — i.e., counter-will — receded into the background.

The tendency to depersonalize the unconscious has been more or less adopted by virtually all subsequent schools of psychoanalysis and adapted to their myriad conceptions of the unconscious. Its explicitly *impersonal* status has persisted while accompanied by technical interventions that emphasize impersonal dimensions to transference phenomena, motivation, and resistance to such a degree that the person engaged in the process has effectively disappeared. Increasingly abstract and ever more arid conceptions of the unconscious have led to more and more impersonal and disassociated conceptions of the transference and the accompanying treatment relationship, and it is understandably this feature of psychoanalysis that existential therapists generally take issue with. Yet the very concept of transference has not been universally embraced by all psychoanalysts. It has even been criticized by some analysts as offering an all-too convenient defense for practitioners who are uncomfortable with the unavoidable *personal engagement* with patients that the intimate psychoanalytic situation usually fosters.

For example, Chertok and de Saussure (1979, cited in Malcolm, 1981, p. 13) argued that Freud's conception of transference often serves, "a defensive measure — a kind of prophylaxis that depersonalizes the relationship and interposes a 'third person' between the patient and the doctor, like the duenna-nurse who peers over the gynecologist's shoulder during examination." Thomas Szasz (1963), back in the days when he was still a psychoanalyst,[3] also alluded to the role of transference as a mode of defense when he observed that "the concept of transference serves two separate analytic purposes: it is a crucial part of the patient's therapeutic experience, and a successful defensive measure to protect the analyst from too intense affective and real-life involvement with the patient" (p. 437). Szasz avers, "the idea of transference implies denial and repudiation of the patient's *experience qua experience*; in its place is substituted the more manageable construct of a *transference experience*" (p. 437). These authors suggest that the analysis of transference is frequently employed to help analysts who are uncomfortable with the personal intimacy aroused between themselves and their patients by attributing such feelings to transference, instead of acknowledging the emotions they genuinely feel for each other.

I suspect that a significant part of the problem derives from our conception of unconscious process and its role in our repression of the personal dimension to the therapy relationship. The term person, or *persona*, was first invoked in Roman law to refer to citizens who possessed the right to vote in a democratic political process. To vote implied an agent who possessed sufficient autonomy to assume responsibility for the decision-making process in which he participated. Because a slave lacked such autonomy he was not deemed a "person" and was accordingly denied the right to vote, as only persons (i.e., non-slaves) were granted these rights. Similarly, Freud, who saw the ego as slave or servant to unconscious processes, decided over time that the unconscious is not personal but impersonal, meaning analytic patients could not be held responsible for acts, thoughts, or intentions they are unconscious of harboring or committing *at the time* they commit them.

Unconscious ideation becomes impersonal precisely when and because it lacks agency. In principle, such thoughts can become personal again (or for the first time) once they become conscious and the person in question accepts responsibility for them. Yet the trend in contemporary psychoanalysis is to maintain the impersonal conception of the so-called transference throughout the therapy experience, no matter how many insights patients may have about the feelings they harbor for their analyst.

The psychoanalytic conception of transference phenomena characterizes the patient's experience of and attributions about the person of the analyst as an inherently *unconscious* process. Efforts by relational analysts to render this dynamic more democratic have subjected the analyst to the same kind of scrutiny as the patient, but the notion of an explicitly personal engagement of the kind I am describing and that falls outside the purview of *technical interventions* is typically rejected. The psychoanalytic literature has consequently tended to focus on transference–countertransference phenomena, their specifically unconscious utility, and the ways that analysts are impacted by their patients' projections. This has led to a consensus that analysts should focus their attention on analyzing such projections while avoiding interactions of a personal nature which, by implication, are defined as *non-interpretative* communications because they do not speak to unconscious processes. To return to the slave metaphor, for relational analysts both analytic patients and their analysts are *equally* enslaved by their respective unconsciouses, in an endless to-and-fro of intersubjectivity and infinite regress.

In other words, all vestiges of the personal relationship shared with patients have been reformulated into aspects of the patient's "transference" with the analyst and the analyst's "countertransference" with the patient, both of which are systematically interpreted and analyzed. From a classical perspective, transference is conceived as a rarefied, trance-like state of childlike hypnotic regression that places the patient in a one-down position from which she cannot extricate herself, because she is always "in" the transference, which she cannot, by definition, escape. This has the chilling consequence of perceiving the therapy patient as never really being the author of his or her experience or a proper adult in an I–Thou relationship, but the "effect" of unconscious forces that only the analyst is privy to. The more recent relational and contemporary effort to extend this process to a similar analysis of the *analyst's* conscious and unconscious process only duplicates the problem, but neither recognizes nor resolves it.

These relatively recent developments fly in the face of a long history of analysts, going all the way back to Freud and Ferenczi, who embrace the concept of a personal or realistic component to the psychoanalytic relationship. Greenson focuses on what he calls the "real" relationship as distinct from the transference, which pertains to perceptions by the patient that are deemed realistic rather than unconscious or defensive. In Greenson's depiction of the real relationship, however, he tends to focus on the patient's experience of the analyst, neglecting the analyst's relationship with the patient. Because the relationship between analyst and patient is not symmetrical, the correlation between their respective positions cannot be identical. Whereas the patient's experience of the analyst is couched in terms of varying degrees of transference phenomena, the analyst's experience of and behavior toward the analysand is typically couched in terms of technique, a circumscribed set of behaviors epitomized by interpretative strategies. The concept of countertransference similarly falls under the purview of technique, whether it is conceived as unconscious impediments to the analyst's optimal functioning in the analytic dyad, or as aspects of the analyst's conscious experience that conform to technical scrutiny. Increasingly, countertransference phenomena are defined simply as the totality of the analyst's experience, including what used to be deemed "personal" reactions, but subsumed under technical oversight, effectively eliminating a genuinely personal, heartfelt component to the relationship.

In other words, most of what the analyst says nowadays is monitored by *technical* considerations, whereas anything of a personal nature — which is to say, anything that is uttered spontaneously and without calculated regard for its intended effect on the patient's transference — is eliminated. Greenson and other analysts who are concerned with distinguishing between transferential and real components of the patient's experience of the process do not specifically address its correlate: *the technical and non-technical components of the analyst's behavior.* It is this aspect of the analyst–patient dyad that I am specifically concerned with in this chapter. The personal *is* the existential, *par excellence.*

Even those relational analysts who object to the classical characterization of the patient's transference as nothing more than distortions of reality tend to conceive virtually all of the analyst's behavior as aspects of technique. For example, Renik (1999) advocates acts of self-disclosure by the analyst and characterizes such revelations as conforming to a technical strategy whose purpose is to exercise a desirable effect on the patient's transference. In such a scheme, the analyst's acts of self-disclosure are not, strictly speaking, personal but rather calculated to have a specific effect. In order for such interventions to be personal they would have to emanate part and parcel from *who* the analyst is, not *what* the analyst does. Renik does not advocate self-disclosure simply because that is who he is and sees no harm in simply being himself. Instead, he specifically contrasts self-disclosure with the idiosyncratic foibles of a given analyst's personality traits and characterizes his self-disclosures as technical interventions. Renik argues that such self-disclosures should be adopted by all analysts, *as a new standard of technique.*

Despite Renik's claim that he is not elevating his personal style to a technique, as soon as he advocates this way of working for *all* analysts he is not suggesting that they be like him, but that they adopt a manner of working — by definition, technique — that he believes will bear greater analytic success. If Renik put his observations down to an attribute of his personality, that this is simply who he is and that he adapts his technique to fit his personality, then he would be explaining how conducting analysis suited *him*, period. But as soon as he advocates his interventions for everyone else to adopt he is advocating a *technical intervention*, which by definition is not personal. As a technique that he advocates for others to follow, it is no longer a character trait but the application of his mind and comportment in the analytic situation.

The Specifically Existential Dimension to the Analytic Relationship

What would behavior of a specifically personal, or existential, nature look like in contrast to a prescribed set of techniques? And how would such behavior be beneficial to the patient's treatment? Am I merely splitting hairs by attempting to distinguish between analytic behavior of a personal rather than technical nature? I don't believe so. The recognition and elaboration of the personal relationship should obviously *enhance* the therapeutic process, not compromise it. Acting from the analyst's person simply for the sake of it would not make much sense if it had a deleterious effect on the treatment relationship. Having said that, if its aim is to benefit the analytic process, then why wouldn't such personal engagement — on a par with Renik's definition of self-disclosure — entail a *technical* intervention, by definition?

The problem with conceptualizing the personal engagement that all analysts experience with their patients as a component of technique is that in order to come across as a genuine person analysts need to be true to their given personality traits and behavioral characteristics, whatever they happen to be. In order to be genuine, the analyst's way of conducting him or herself should be natural, spontaneous, and without guile. The most common complaint patients typically make about analysts who conform to classical technique is the *lack of genuineness* concerning the way they conduct themselves.[4] Yet, one of the principal goals of analytic treatment is to increase the patient's capacity for genuineness in their manner of relating to others, as well as themselves. Those analysts who object to a classical or austere way of behaving with patients and advocate doing the opposite, e.g., affecting a more conversational and emotional engagement with their patients, invariably argue that *all* analysts would be advised to behave that way, even if such a way of behaving feels out of character or unnatural to a given analyst. It is my impression that most analysts are not naturally talkative nor do they wear their hearts on their sleeves. For them, being "themselves" might well entail remaining silent throughout most of their analytic sessions, not because their technique tells them to, but because that is what they are comfortable doing, with more of less everyone. To become talkative and responsive would not only feel unnatural to them, it would also be experienced by their patients as contrived and artificial, perhaps weird. Winnicott is a perfect example of an analyst who learned over many years the value of saying little, yet was regarded by all who saw him in treatment as uncommonly considerate and genuine. Analysts typically connect with their patients in ways they are not entirely aware of because, in so doing, they are just being themselves, whatever that entails. By extension, an analyst cannot be him or herself and conceive doing so as a *standard of technique*. Being oneself is, by definition, personal. As such, it is an act of creativity that is *uniquely one's own*.

So what are the criteria for being oneself that most analysts find so objectionable that it has been factored out of the psychoanalytic treatment perspective? Unlike the techniques that analysts adopt, *there cannot be universal standards* for how a given analyst uses his or her personality in the treatment of each patient. Freud wasn't even comfortable with mandating strict standards for his technical principles, let alone the personal ones! As a rule of thumb, what is deemed personal — what I am defining as existential — is basically common-sensical, if not immediately predictable or obvious. It is both outside technique and subject to individual variation. It cannot be codified because, just as analysts differ from person to person, each analyst's conception of the personal relationship will vary accordingly. Moreover, analysts are liable to form different conceptions of what the personal relationship entails at different stages of their careers and with different patients, when they succumb to this or that mood, the time of day, how long they have been working with a given patient, and so on.

For the personal relationship to be spontaneous, unpredictable, and authentic it has to be free of contrivance and subterfuge, a manner of being that, for lack of a better word, comes from the heart. This is why the most common incidence of the personal relationship is often manifested in the form of *spontaneous conversations* that evolve between analyst and patient. Such conversations may include self-disclosures by the analyst, but not necessarily. The basic idea is that not everything the analyst says is limited to offering interpretations, eliciting data, or other technical considerations. Classical analysts tend to reject conversation out of hand because they believe "conversing" has no discernable role in the analytic process, whereas relational analysts tend to reduce such otherwise spontaneous conversations to a technique that can come across as contrived and manipulative. Conversations are obviously gratifying for patient and analyst alike and are necessarily restrained by the use of abstinence, but to abandon them entirely becomes artificial for those analysts who, like Freud and Ferenczi, were naturally conversational. For example, there are times when patients may want to muse about ideas, whether literary, philosophical, or spiritual, when reflecting on the human condition and their place in the scheme of things, and ask their analysts to reciprocate. Analysts may in turn participate in such conversations without the need to reduce such musings to manifestations of transference and analyze them accordingly. Some analysts may even initiate such conversations when the spirit moves them to, for reasons that are not necessarily apparent to them at the time. It is my sense that such spontaneous, inherently extra-analytic exchanges have a profound impact on the analytic relationship as well as the outcome of the therapy, but in ways that we may be incapable of determining on a case-by-case basis, let alone moment-to-moment.

Permitting one's personality to become part of the constellation of elements that analysts utilize serves as an invaluable source for authentic relating with patients. *It is my thesis that these incidents of feeling genuinely connected to one's analyst are critical, if unconventional, even controversial, components of every successful treatment experience*, and the *sine qua non* of the existential perspective. Because each analyst's personality is unique, each analyst's manner of being personally engaged with patients will vary. Feeling free to converse spontaneously is only one personality trait among many that cannot be reduced to technical edicts. For example, a given analyst's capacity for affection, disaffection, concern, kindness, courage, consideration, compassion, curiosity, and wisdom are all personal characteristics that will fundamentally differ from one analyst to another. Moreover, such characteristics cannot be taught in psychoanalytic institutes, nor can they be learned in supervision. You might say they are so personal that each analyst has to struggle in her own analysis to discover which ones epitomize the peculiarities of her own personality, and determine those that are strengths and weaknesses and develop her clinical style accordingly. They are not only traits of personality, but part and parcel aspects of the analyst's *way of being* and operative in all aspects of it, including the relationships that are fashioned with one's patients.

The Role of Character in the Existential Relationship

Of all the psychoanalytic perspectives that have emphasized the role of the personal relationship, the interpersonal and existential perspectives are the most explicit in addressing this aspect of the analyst–analysand relationship. This is not to suggest that other perspectives have neglected this issue. On the contrary, there is a rich psychoanalytic literature that both addresses and advocates the role of the personal relationship in the analytic process, as I noted above.[5] The existential tradition has even questioned the efficacy of making clear-cut distinctions between the personal and transference relationships.[6] Existentialists have historically tended to avoid terms like technique and focus instead on those phenomena that the patient is aware of and those that the patient is not aware of, that which is accessible to awareness and that which is inaccessible.[7] The fact that analysts occupy a necessarily professional role in their work does not necessarily imply that the relationship fashioned with their patients is not an inherently personal one. Yes, there are professional relationships that do not occasion a personal dimension. For example, x-ray technicians in a hospital setting may have little if any opportunity to engage in personal conversation with their subjects because they can carry out their role with minimal if any personal contact. Psychoanalytic relationships, however, cannot avoid such contact because the personal medium of engaging in conversation is the *essence* of their professional activities. The boundaries between the personal and professional are constantly evolving in ways we are not entirely aware of.

It should be apparent by now that the character, or person, of a given analyst is of critical importance to how that analyst's patients will experience and benefit from that relationship.

Whereas technical *principles* are indispensable to every kind of therapy, the question I am addressing is the often neglected but equally important issue of the therapist's (whether psychoanalytic or otherwise) unique personality and attendant character traits. For some analysts — and I would include myself among them — the role of the analyst's character is of far greater importance than the technique a given analyst opts to employ. There is no way of empirically substantiating this claim but I believe it, nevertheless. All I can is that after more than forty years of clinical practice, this is how it seems to me.

That being said, the psychoanalytic conception of character has been historically pathologized as embedded structures of the personality that compromise the individual's ability to obtain maximum gratification from or adaptation to life. Freud employed the word "character" in two distinct ways. In his earlier writings (but also sporadically in later papers) he referred to character in the sense of a virtuous, upstanding individual, but the vast majority of his publications refer to character in the second sense, as a form of psychopathology that is deeply embedded in the patient's personality. The first to catch Freud's attention was the obsessional type, soon followed by a host of others and subsequently expanded on by a succession of new generations of analysts. Because they are so deeply embedded the individual is profoundly adapted to a given constellation of character types, e.g., hysterical, obsessive, schizoid, borderline, narcissistic, paranoid, and so on. The notion that character may refer to features of one's personality structure that are inherently *virtuous* is not a typical preoccupation of contemporary psychoanalytic literature or nomenclature. We speak in an off-hand way of a person possessing good character or strong character to signify an individual of exemplary moral fiber who epitomizes excellent virtues, such as the ones I listed above, e.g., kindness, generosity, courage, integrity, honesty, resolve, and the like. But these examples of character are usually invoked only when employing non-technical terminology about the patient, somehow outside the analyst–patient dynamic.

Though Freud referred to his first use of character only fleetingly (see, for example, Freud, 1905 [1953]), he never abandoned his belief that virtuous character traits are an indelible ingredient of every successful analytic treatment. He perceived the British, for example, as a culture he admired for possessing "excellent" character. Moreover, he believed that candidates for analytic treatment should possess a degree of good character, but the precise character traits they should exhibit are left for us to ponder. Since Freud, analysts have tended to remain silent about such expectations. As the treatment of severe psychopathologies (e.g., schizoid, narcissistic, and borderline character structure especially) has increasingly dominated the psychoanalytic literature the question of analyzability has receded into the background. Freud questioned whether schizoid and narcissistic patients could be analyzed because he believed they were too self-absorbed; yet this assessment was based on their pathology, not their character, specifically. Freud's focus, as we know, was on neurotics (hysteria and obsessional neurosis), yet many of them he deemed "good for nothing" and unsuitable for the kind of perseverance, honesty, and good will that he expected analytic patients to embody. These character traits were, in his way of thinking, independent of the pathology (whether neurotic or psychotic) a given patient suffers.

Similarly, Freud (1913 [1958]) expected analysts to possess an even higher degree of virtue than the patients they treat, most prominent among them honesty.[8] Freud didn't say a lot about honesty because it is not a matter of technique but concerns the analyst's personality. He or she has got it or hasn't, but it cannot be turned on or off like a switch or learned via a course of study. Moreover, analysts who do not possess a high degree of character will find the trials and demands of analytic work not to their liking. They may very well succeed in becoming analysts, but it was Freud's opinion they will not be very good at it because they will serve as poor role models for their patients. Until recently analytic institutes typically assessed for character in screening prospective applicants for training, but increasingly this question is omitted from consideration because character is so difficult to measure and depends more or less entirely on the subjective opinion of the analysts conducting the interviews.[9] Ironically, in order to make the admissions process less subjective and more democratic the relevance of and preoccupation about the relation between the analyst's character and technique has receded into the background.

Even if personal virtue cannot be taught, the concept can be and should be included in the curriculum of psychoanalytic institutes. Though we cannot "learn" to be virtuous, we can raise our awareness to those aspects of our personalities that disclose our attitudes about our work and inherent frustrations and the role our character plays even in many of our notions about theory and technique, the kinds of patients we like to work with and those we do not. Given the vast amount of literature on character pathology, it would also be instructive to distinguish between the two types of character I have been discussing, including their relationship to personality (now employed more or less interchangeably with character) and what I have been depicting as the personal relationship.

Existential Psychoanalysis Versus Existential Therapy

I have used this chapter so far to distinguish the most important features of what differentiates existential psychoanalysis from the other schools of psychoanalysis, specifically the lack of a personal dimension in conventional psychoanalytic practice. So what are the distinguishing features that differentiate existential psychoanalysis from existential *therapies* that are explicitly non-psychodynamic?

In reviewing virtually all schools of existential therapy,[10] they tend to reject diagnostic considerations (e.g., neurotic, hysterical, narcissistic, borderline, psychotic, etc.), transference and countertransference phenomena and any allusion to unconscious processes. This represents a virtual rejection of the basic premises upon which psychoanalysis, as a distinctive school of psychotherapy, is founded. Contrast this with the work of R. D. Laing, whose first two books, *The Divided Self* (1960 [1969]) and *Self and Others* (1961 [1969]) are existential critiques of psychoanalysis as well as a concerted study of schizophrenia and schizoid phenomena. Is there anything wrong with this? No, not really. As I noted earlier, all forms of psychotherapy are helpful and no one school of psychotherapy is demonstrably or inherently better than any other. It depends on what a prospective patient is looking for and whether the type of therapy that person is seeking is appropriate. In my opinion psychoanalysis generally, including existential psychoanalysis, offers more depth in its undertaking. This is because it is usually a lengthy affair that does not always lend itself to short term or brief interventions. However, I am all too well aware that my existential therapy colleagues would argue that their reliance on existential philosophy, which virtually all schools of psychoanalysis ignore, offers a degree of depth that is lacking among psychoanalysts. This comes down to a matter of opinion, but I see their point. Rollo May once confided to me that he felt psychoanalysts who are not philosophically trained "do not see the big picture, because they are too embedded in minutiae" (personal communication, 1985).

Excepting Rollo May and Irvin Yalom, none of the leading lights of existential therapy (e.g., Kirk Schneider, Emmy van Deurzen, Ernesto Spinelli, Del Loewenthal, Victor Frankl) adopt psychoanalytic nomenclature or principles. In fact, many existential therapists feel that their approach has more in common with cognitive behavioral and humanistic therapies than with psychoanalysis, the former because of its emphasis on conscious and deliberate experience (as opposed to unconscious and indirect phenomena) and the latter due to its emphasis on pursuing the good life instead of focusing on psychopathology. As I noted above, it all depends on what you are looking for.

I know by this point, as we are nearing our conclusion, you are wondering why I have not offered any clinical vignettes to demonstrate how existential psychoanalysts work with their patients. What is their clinical technique? What, for example, sets the techniques of existential psychoanalysts apart from those of existential therapists, as well as the various schools of psychoanalysis? Existential psychoanalysis, as I conceive it, has no inherent theory, nor does it have a technique. Given its nature, it is up to each psychoanalyst to select which psychoanalyst or analysts they draw from, and which existential philosopher or philosophers are also relevant to their predilections. For myself, I draw mainly from Freud and R. D. Laing among the analysts who have influenced me, and to a lesser degree Winnicott, Bion, and Lacan. Among the existential philosophers that I draw from are Sartre, Nietzsche, and Heidegger. Plato, Aristotle, and the skeptics are also important influences in my thinking and development as an existential psychoanalyst. As you have seen, these are the sources that I cite in this book and who comprise the influences I draw from.

There is no necessary or fundamental analyst or philosopher that one is obliged to draw from, but naturally one would have to select from analysts who are compatible with an existential orientation. I do not believe, for example, that Melanie Klein is compatible with an existential framework, but again that is up to each practitioner to determine. This is why any theoretical perspective would necessarily be idiosyncratic. As for technique, given the nature of the beast, the closest I can get to anything resembling technical principals are broad. I draw on Freud and his papers on technique to guide me. In fact, I have published two books on my existential interpretation of Freud's technical principles, *The Truth About Freud's Technique* (1994) and *The Ethic of Honesty* (2004), each of which are detailed reviews of Freud's technical principles.

I wish I could share with you a typical analytic session that would demonstrate how I work, but I have no typical sessions to share. There aren't any. Each session is unique. I have tried to explain that I am very informal, relaxed, conversational, and direct. This says more about my character than about any kind of circumscribed "technique" that I might follow. *I have been trying to explain in this chapter that it is the character of the analyst, who the analyst **is**, not what the analyst **does**, specifically, that determines the efficacy of a given analyst's treatment philosophy, out of which his or her clinical decorum will follow.* This follows on Freud's recommendation that every analyst should apply technique to their personality, and should *not* conform their personality to a technique. I have followed these recommendations to the letter. In a way, you could say that I simply wing it, and follow my intuition and four decades of clinical experience. This also follows from my former mentor and teacher, R. D. Laing, the psychoanalyst who virtually invented existential psychoanalysis in its current form, but who never addressed his clinical philosophy or interventions or vignettes in any of his publications. When I asked him why, he said that if he gave any concrete examples of how he conducted a therapy session, no matter what he said, the reader would inevitably read into his case report an example of how every therapy session should be conducted, and turn it into a regimen that must be followed to the letter. Instead, Laing chose to conduct his teaching and training in the context of the psychoanalytic training school he founded in London, the *Philadelphia Association*. My own school, *New School for Existential Psychoanalysis*, located in San Francisco, follows the same model.

In conclusion, the capacity to acknowledge the existence of a personal relationship with one's patients, and the wherewithal to freely engage it in a manner that complements the specific needs of each treatment situation, lends a dimension of genuineness and authenticity to the relationship that has profound implications for the way the analysis is experienced, and even how technical principles are applied. Fortunately, most analysts know this intuitively — if not deliberately — and conduct themselves accordingly.

Notes

1 Though this term is rarely invoked nowadays, it has been replaced here and there with terms such as the personal or real relationship, or the working or therapeutic alliance.
2 Interpretations enjoy a wide and diverse application. It is up to each analyst to decide which ones to privilege. Freud favored genetic interpretations, connecting early childhood experiences with current situations. Other analysts favor transference interpretations: "Everything you say is really about me." Others privilege defense mechanisms, "resistance." Their focus is on the variety of ways that you may have lost focus on the analytic work at hand. And then there is the question of how much you want to engage in interpretations in the first place.
3 Szasz became so frustrated with psychoanalysis that he eventually turned against it and psychotherapy more generally, due to his rejection of the concept of "mental illness," which therapists claim to treat.
4 For an illuminating example of such complaints, see Daphne Merkin, 2010, pp. 28–47.
5 For example, see Ticho, 1982; Ticho and Richards, 1982; Gill, 1988; Gitelson, 1962, 1952; A. Reich, 1958; Bouvet, 1958; Nacht, 1958.
6 See Laing, 1967 [1983]; Tillich, 2000; and Buber, 1970 for informed discussions concerning the personal nature of every therapeutic encounter.
7 See Askey and Farquhar, 2006, for an illuminating review of existentialist and phenomenological critiques of the unconscious.
8 See Thompson, 2004, for more on Freud's views about honesty.

9 Unfortunately, this practice was also abused. Until relatively recently women and homosexuals were excluded from consideration because they were deemed to possess poor character!
10 I exclude the work of Rollo May and Irvin Yalom for reasons I discussed earlier. Rollo May was a trained psychoanalyst, though none of his publications would hint at this due to his disenchantment with the lack of interest within the psychoanalytic community in existential philosophy. Yalom trained with May and adopted some of the latter's inherent debt to psychoanalytic principles, including diagnostic considerations and allusions to unconscious and transference phenomena.

References

Askey, R. and Farquhar, J. (2006) *Apprehending the inaccessible: Freudian psychoanalysis and existential phenomenology*. Evanston, IL: Northwestern University Press.

Bouvet, M. (1958) Technical variation and the concept of distance. *International Journal of Psychoanalysis*, Volume 39: 211–221.

Buber, M. (1970) *I and thou* (W. Kaufman, trans.). New York: Free Press.

Davies, J. and Frawley, M. (1991) Dissociative processes and transference–countertransference paradigms in psychoanalytically oriented treatment of adult survivors of childhood sexual abuse. In S. Mitchell and L. Aron (Eds.), *Relational psychoanalysis: The emergence of a tradition*. Hillsdale, NJ: The Analytic Press.

Freud, S. (1905 [1953]) On psychotherapy. *Standard edition*, 7: 257–268. London: Hogarth Press.

Freud, S. (1913 [1958]) On beginning the treatment (further recommendations on the technique of psycho-analysis I). *Standard edition*, 12: 121–144. London: Hogarth Press.

Freud, S. (1915 [1958]) Observations on transference-love (further recommendations on the technique of psycho-analysis III). *Standard edition*, 12: 157–171. London: Hogarth Press.

Gill, M. (1988) Converting psychotherapy into psychoanalysis. *Contemporary Psychoanalysis*, Volume 24, No. 2: 262–274.

Gitelson, M. (1952) The emotional position of the analyst in the psychoanalytic situation. *International Journal of Psychoanalysis*, Volume 33: 1–10.

Gitelson, M. (1962) The curative factors in psycho-analysis. *International Journal of Psychoanalysis*, Volume 43, No. 4–5, 194–205.

Haynal, A. (1997) A European view: A Meeting of Minds: Mutuality in Psychoanalysis by Lewis Aron (Hillsdale, NJ: The Analytic Press, 1996). *Psychoanalytic Dialogues*, Volume 7: 881–884.

Hoffman, I. (1983) The patient as interpreter of the analyst's experience. In S. Mitchell and L. Aron (Eds.), *Relational psychoanalysis: The emergence of a tradition*. Hillsdale, NJ: The Analytic Press.

Laing, R. D. 1960 [1969]) *The divided self*. New York and London: Penguin Books.

Laing, R. D. (1961 [1969]) *Self and others*. New York and London: Penguin Books.

Laing, R. D. (1967 [1983]) *The politics of experience*. New York: Pantheon.

Leavy, S. (1988) *In the image of God: A psychoanalyst's view*. New Haven and London: Yale University Press.

Malcolm, J. (1981) *Psychoanalysis: The impossible profession*. New York: Alfred A. Knoph.

Maroda, K. J. (2007) Ethical considerations of the home office. *Psychoanalytic Psychology*, Volume 24: 173–179.

Merkin, D. (2010) My life in therapy: What 40 years of talking to analysts has taught me. *The New York Times Magazine*, August 8.

Mitchell, S. and Black, M. (1995) *Freud and beyond: A history of modern psychoanalytic thought*. New York: Basic Books.

Nacht, S. (1958) Variations in technique. *International Journal of Psychoanalysis*, Volume 39: 235–237.

Ogden, T. (1994) The analytic third: Working with intersubjective clinical facts. In S. Mitchell and L. Aron (Eds.), *Relational psychoanalysis: The emergence of a tradition*. Hillsdale, NJ: The Analytic Press.

Reich, A. (1958) A special variation of technique. *International Journal of Psychoanalysis*, Volume 39: 230–234.

Renik, O. (1999) Playing one's cards face up in analysis: An approach to the problem of self-disclosure. *The Psychoanalytic Quarterly*, Volume 68: 521–539.

Szasz, T. (1963) The concept of transference. *The International Journal of Psychoanalysis*, Volume 44: 432–443.

Thompson, M. G. (1994) *The truth about Freud's technique: The encounter with the real*. New York and London: New York University Press.

Thompson, M. G. (2004) *The ethic of honesty: The fundamental rule of psychoanalysis*. Amsterdam and New York: Rodopi.

Ticho, E. (1982) The alternate schools of the self. *Journal of the American Psychoanalytic Association*, Volume 30: 840–862.

Ticho, E. and Richards, A. (1982) Psychoanalytic theories of the self. *Journal of the American Psychoanalytic Association*, Volume 30: 717–733.

Tillich, P. (2000) *The courage to be*. New Haven, CT and London: Yale University Press.

Conclusion

In closing, I want to address possible criticisms that may be weighed against existential psychoanalysis as I have outlined it in this book.

I believe that the most resistance some practitioners may have with this school of psychoanalysis is the way that it dispenses with the notion of *causality* in the etiology of so-called pathological symptoms, whether hysteria, obsessional neurosis, borderline personality disorder, narcissism, psychosis, paranoia, and so on. The conventional view is that something or someone in our childhood treated us in such a way that it "caused" a traumatic event which in turn caused the symptoms of anxiety, depression, or unhappiness that patients typically bring our attention to in the early stages of their therapy. Others feel that genetic factors may also be in play, perhaps predominantly so. Some believe that the diagnosis of schizophrenia, for example, is the consequence of having been born with a predilection to over-sensitivity to one's environment, triggered in turn by a toxic environmental factor, e.g., an abusive mother, an absent father, a broken marriage and family life. In other words, that some *trauma* or other must have caused us to become neurotic, or psychotic, or whatever, even allowing for genetic factors. Trauma, or PTSD, is perhaps the most prevalent concept that we see today in nearly all the mental health professions, in the media, on the internet, virtually everywhere. For the existentialist, however, nothing has "caused" me to be this way or that. In effect, I — no doubt unconsciously — *chose* to be this way or that.

This thesis will be roundly rejected by conventional psychoanalysts, because they are wedded to the notion that the traumatic nature of our early environment is precisely what causes us to develop the symptoms that bring us into therapy. This thesis will also be rejected by the vast majority of existential therapists, simply because they do not believe in the unconscious, so how in the world can we "unconsciously" choose our symptoms, our neuroses? Or worse, if choice is an inherently *conscious* affair, how can it be committed with deliberation and aforethought? How can this make any sense? But this is precisely what the existential psychoanalyst is proposing, the same thesis that I outlined in Chapter Two: "Sartre and Psychoanalysis." There I explained, from an existential psychoanalytic perspective, that nothing "causes" us to succumb to our symptoms, neither genetic nor environmental, because due to our inherent freedom we effectively choose our neuroses and all the other pathological symptoms we happen to suffer. This thesis is not inherent in all existential theories, but it is essential to the philosophy of Jean-Paul Sartre (1943 [1954]), Maurice Merleau-Ponty (1962), and Martin Heidegger (2001), which any existential psychoanalyst who has been influenced by them consequently adopts. There is no way to prove whether trauma theory or its alternative, unconscious choice, is correct. It is simply a matter of how we see things, and whether seeing it this way or that is amenable to my understanding of the world.

This is the core of the problem that all therapists face, whether they are wedded to psychoanalysis, cognitive behavior therapy, Rogerian therapy, and even existential therapy. Psychotherapy of any persuasion is not an empirical science. Despite all the claims about "empirical outcomes" of this or that type of psychotherapy, their efficacy rests entirely on an article of faith. You have your experience as a practitioner, the school of therapy you are wedded to, but we cannot possibly know what the effectiveness of this or that kind of therapy is. Yet, despite this, we adopt a given style of therapy to practice, and we make the most of it, hoping to help our patients as much as we can. Yes, we refine the way we work over time, and we like to say that we learn from our mistakes, but the outcome of any kind of psychotherapy is ultimately in the hands of the patient. Outcome is mysterious, and despite all the studies that have been published claiming to be the most effective, there is virtually no proof that this is so.

I know that saying this will stir controversy, perhaps outrage among my colleagues. But it is what I believe. What I am offering in this argument is an inherently skeptical approach to the problem: we simply do not have all the answers as practitioners. We are all flying by the seat of our pants. Existentialists are skeptics at heart, and they know that the pursuit of truth is a complicated affair, one that challenges us every day. The wherewithal to accommodate this ambiguity, and embrace the uncertainty of our task, is the epitome of existential psychoanalysis.

I know I haven't provided a perfectly crafted encapsulation of what the term *existential*, nor for that matter *existential psychoanalysis*, means. I have alluded to it, and perhaps that is the only authentic way of approaching the matter, by allusion. I hope I have at least provided an appetizer, a taste of more to come. As I have argued, psychoanalysis, in its latency, *has always been* existential, in the manner that Freud conceived it, and how I have developed it further. There is no existential theory, nor an existential technique, for there can never be anything remotely resembling an existential "how to" book by the numbers. Given its inchoate nature, existentialism, and any derivative approach to therapy, can never be articulated from a theoretical perspective that will meet universal agreement. This is why existential psychoanalysis can only ever be rooted in a *sensibility* which, in turn, is based on a manner of being with another person that helps the practitioner adopt an open-minded way of being with others.

When all is said and done, the existentialist sensibility is nothing more than a style of engagement that is at once personal and elusive, that haunts every moment of the time we allot ourselves to engage in that most mysterious and perplexing of callings, the therapeutic process.

References

Heidegger, M. (2001) *Zollikon seminars* (F. Mayr and R. Askay, trans.) Evanston, IL: Northwestern University Press.

Merleau-Ponty, M. (1962) *Phenomenology of perception* (C. Smith, trans.). London: Routledge and Kegan Paul.

Sartre, J.-P. (1943 [1954]) *Being and nothingness* (H. Barnes, trans.). New York: Philosophical Library.

Index

509th Radio Research Group, involvement 15

abstinence (Freud technical recommendation) 11, 58; understanding, problem 61
actions, fiction (playing) 38–39
Adler, Alfred 1
affection, analyst capacity 96–97
affect, term (psychoanalysis adaptation) 35
agency, abdication 62
Alanson White Institute 18
Alexander, Franz 70
alienation: existentialism, association 7; relief 58, 62; sense 54–55
Allen, Woody 4
American ego psychology 83
analysis: analytic patient introduction 59; goal 43–44; rule 58
analysts: attentiveness, diversion 71; behavior, technical/non-technical components 93; capacity 96–97; efficacy 83; interventions, impact (absence) 62; open-mindedness 59; patient narcissistic relationship, upset 65; personality traits, impact 93; self-disclosure 95–96; virtue, expectation (Freud) 99
analytic candidates, selection process 71
analytic discourse, personal relationship (elimination) 71
analytic hour, patient obsessional control 65
analytic interventions, minimum (encouragement) 70–71
analytic process, deprivation chamber (analysis) 61
analytic relationship: specifically existential dimension 94–97; working alliance, problems 72
analytic treatment, goal 94–95
Angel, Ernest 19; *Existence: A New Dimension in Psychiatry and Psychology* 19
anger, knowledge (absence) 33–34
angst: experience/constancy 15–16; feeling 13–14; term, usage 6–7
anxiety: contention (Freud) 6–7; increase 9; necessity, Nietzsche/Heidegger perspective 54–55; production 52; symptoms 106
Arendt, Hannah 4
Aristotle: honesty perspective 57–58; influence 101–102
Army Security Agency, assignation 14–15
artificiality, fostering 72
attitudes, identification 53

authentic act (Heidegger) 52–53
authentic hero, epitomization 46–47
authenticity: allusion 43; application 66; characterization 47; conception, adoption/rejection 49; conception (Heidegger), origin 51–52; example 64; Freud 55–62; impact 40; Nietzsche/Heidegger 45–55; notion (Heidegger), contrast 46–47; postmodernist rejection 53–54; problem 7; promotion 6; psychoanalytic experience, relationship 62–66; rule 62; transference-countertransference relationship, link 66–75; unconventionality/difficulty/genuineness 45; usage, avoidance 44; vicissitudes 43
authenticity, concept: attributes 45; evidence, search 53–54; implicitness 45; issues 44–45
authentic self-identity 54
autonomy, absence 90–91

Bacon, Francis 4
bad faith (Sartre) 31; impact 34; problem, resolution (failure) 32
Beauvoir, Simone de 3, 13, 26
Beckett, Samuel 4
behavior, attribute 45
behaviorism, problems 37
Being and Nothingness (Sartre) 2, 4, 26, 28
Being and Time (Heidegger) 4, 5, 47, 52–53
Bergman, Ingmar 4
Bergmann, Martin 11
Binswanger, Ludwig: existential analysis 19; *Psychoanalysis and Daseinanalysis* 19; psychoanalysis, integration attempt 19

Bion, Wilfried 11, 21, 44, 64, 66; transference, nature (insights) 65
Blake, William 4
borderline personality disorder 106
boredom, feeling 13–14
Boss, Medard (psychoanalysis, integration attempt) 18
Boulder Psychotherapy Institute (Cannon) 20
bourgeois, Sartre contempt 28
British School of Existential Analysis (van Deurzen/Spinelli) 20
Buber, Martin 4
Buddhism 7, 16
Buddhist meditation 50
Bunuel, Luis 4

Café de Flore 3
Camus, Albert (*The Stranger*) 4
Cannon, Betty 20
Capote, Truman 15
Cartesian ego 48–49
Catholicism, confession (importance) 12
causality, notion 106
Cezanne, Paul 4
change, concept (approach) 29
character: role 97–100; traits, identification 53; traits, uniqueness 98
childlike hypnotic regression 72, 91
choice: conscious choice, impact 38; consequences 40; free choice, absence 39; freedom (Heidegger) 38; freedom, relationship 38–41; occurrence, pre-reflective level 38; unconscious aspect 55; volitional choice 38
City Lights Book Store 16
Civilization and Its Discontents (Freud) 47, 56
classical analyst: extra-analytic engagement rejection 72; stereotype 61

classical technique 75
cognitive behavioral therapy (CBT) 88
Cold War, impact 5
common unhappiness, transformation 43
comprehension, impact 31
concern, analyst capacity 96–97
condition: cause, absence 40; change 56
confession, importance 12
conscious apprehension 33
conscious choice, impact 38
consciousness: intentionality 32; knowledge, implication (absence) 33–34; second consciousness, model 31; unity 33
consciousness-*of* something 32
consideration, analyst capacity 96–97
contrivance, absence 73–74
conversation, avoidance 74
countertransference: example 60; features 65; transference, relationship 45, 66
courage, analyst capacity 96
Cuban Missile Crisis 14
Cuba, revolution 15–16
curiosity, analyst capacity 96
cynicism 15

Dali, Salvador 4
Dark Night of the Soul, The (St. John of the Cross) 8
Dasein, usage 49–50
Death of Desire: an Existential Study in Sanity and Madness (Thompson) 22, 82
defense mechanisms 89
depression: increase 9; struggle 14; symptoms 106
Descartes, René (tangible self conception) 48
desire: erasure 65; structure 37

deterministic processes, impact 36
diagnosis, phenomenon (existential therapy rejection) 22
diagnostic categories, conception (Freud) 22
Dick, Philip K. 4, 7
disaffection, analyst capacity 96–97
disillusionment 62; usage 63
dislocation, feeling 13–14
distortions (transference phenomena) 85
distress, consequence 64
Divided Self, The (Laing) 16–17, 28, 100
divorce, experience 14
Dostoyevsky, Fyodor 4

ego: conscious portion 31; unconscious portion 31
Ellenberger, H.F. 19; *Existence: A New Dimension in Psychiatry and Psychology* 19
emotions: definition, theories (multitude) 34–35; desire structure 37; escape 36–37; intelligence, presence 36; self-destructiveness 36; term, adaptation 35
emotions, critique (Sartre) 34–37
émouvoir (emotions) 35
empathy, problem (Husserl preoccupation) 51
enactments, term (introduction) 83
environment: humans, connection 7; over-sensitivity, predilection 106; traumatic nature 107
envy, knowledge (absence) 33–34
epistemology, impact 31
epoché, initiation (Pyrrho) 9
Erikson, Erik 84
erotic transference 69
Ethic of Honesty, the (Thompson) 102
executive function, discussion (absence) 39

Existence: A New Dimension in Psychiatry and Psychology (May/Angel/Ellenberger) 19
existential: technical term 2; term, meaning/usage 1, 10
existential analysis, naming (Binswanger) 19
existential crisis 13–14
existential encapsulation 108
Existential-Humanistic Institute (Schneider) 17, 20
existentialism: alienation, association 7; articulation, problem 23; creation 2–3; defining 5; development, philosophers (involvement) 3–4; Heidegger, importance 3–4; origins 9; popularity 7–8; psychoanalysis, relationship 26
existential phenomenology 34
existential philosophers, impact 20
existential psychoanalysis: conversational approach 11–12; curative power 12; defining 1; differences 18–19; existential therapy, contrast 18–23, 100–103; goal 40–41; invention (Laing) 102–103; nodal point 74; psychoanalysis, distinctions 20–21; terms, identification 44–45
existential relationship, character (role) 97–100
existential therapy: differentiation 100; non-psychoanalytic schools 11
existential therapy, flexibility 2
existing, manner 51
experience: meaning 33; meaning, association 5; term, usage 5
experiencing self, envisionment 48
extra-analytic engagement, classical analyst rejection 72
extra-transference 66; relationship 45

factual reality, psychic reality (contrast) 29
Fairbairn, Ronald 84
fallenness (Verfallenheit), incidence 47
family therapy 88
Fanon, Franz 4
fantasies: experience (Freud) 30; purpose 30; treatment 30
feelings, consciousness 34
feeling-sefl, notion 48
feeling-states 48–49
Fellini, Federico 4
Fenichel, Ann 74
Ferenczi, Sandor 61–62, 84
Ferlinghetti, Lawrence 16
Frankl, Viktor 20, 101
free association 59–60; Freud technical recommendation 11; interference 60–61
Free Association, Inc. 20
free choice 40; absence 39
freedom: choice, relationship 38–41; conception (Sartre) 29; impact 39
Freudian analysts, technique 68
Freud, Sigmund 74, 84; attention 98; authenticity 55–62; Binswanger/Boss, affiliation 19; case reports, interventions (reporting absence) 67–68; *Civilization and Its Discontents* 47, 56; diagnostic categories, conception 22; existential perspective 11; fantasies, experience 30; followers, break 1; formulations, Sartre formulations (difference) 34; good, human pursuit 57; influence 101; love, emphasis 21; psychic reality, conception 29–30; psychoanalysis: creation 1; depiction 31; Sartre, relationship 28; sex, obsession 28; sexuality, emphasis 1; structural

model 89; *Studies on Hysteria* 76; superego conception 63; technical interventions 68–69; technical recommendations 58; therapeutic ambition 60; *Three Essays on the Theory of Sexuality* 12; topographical model, Sartre rejection 31; transference conception 63, 90; traumatic moment 36; treatment philosophy 45; tri-partite structure 39; unconscious: conception 29; theory 29; topographical model 29
Fromm, Erich 11, 84
Fromm-Reichmann, Frieda 11, 73
frustration, consequence 64

Gegenwille (counter-will), term (coining) 89
genuineness: absence 94; dimension 75
God, belief 8
good, human pursuit (Freud) 57
Greek skeptics, knowledge acquisition (overcoming) 48
Greenson, Ralph 85
guile, absence 73–74
guilt, impact 63

Hammett, Dashiell 4
happiness: conception, method 57; promise 56
Hegel, Georg Wilhelm Friedrich 3
Heidegger, Martin 107; authenticity 45–55; authenticity, conception (origin) 51; *Being and Time* 4, 5, 47, 52–53; choice, freedom 38; embracing 28; existentialism, importance 3–4; Greeks, impact 10; impact 26; motivations, knowledge (impossibility) 55; philosophy, adaptation 16; philosophy, Nietzsche/Kierkegaard source 45–46; psychoanalysis, integration attempt 19; unconscious, examination 31
Hemingway, Ernest 4, 14, 26–27; meeting/friendship 13; non-conformism 27
hermeneutics 44
Heuscher, Julius 20
hidden/true self 48–49
Hitchcock, Alfred 4
honesty: authenticity 57–58; capacity 57–58; capacity, requirement/ enhancement 43; value 6
human condition: assessment 19; attention 21
human endeavor, origin (Greek beliefs) 10
humanistic therapy 88
humans, estrangement 7
Husserl, Edmund 4, 32; empathy, problem 51; phenomenology 9
hypnotic regression 72, 91
hysteria 99, 106
hysterical misery, transformation 43, 63

id: decision-making ability 39; knowledge 31; language 89
idealization 75
inauthentic course, selection (non-neurotic reasons) 63
inauthenticity 60; Heidegger 53–54; process, analyst mistrust 60–61; Sartre 31; source 68
indirection, impact 41
infantile fixations 75
instrumentality 72
intentionality, definition (Sartre) 32
interpersonal psychoanalysis, creation 18
intersubjectivity 44; theory. *see* theory of intersubjectivity.
intimacy: fear, overcoming 40; obtaining 72

invulnerability, patient abandonment 43, 63–64
I-Thou relationship 92

Jaspers, Karl 4
Journal of Existential Psychiatry and Psychology, emergence 19–20
Jung, C.G. 1; Binswanger/Boss, affiliation 19

Kafka, Franz 4
Kennedy, John F. 14
Kerouac, Jack 16
Kesey, Ken 16
keyholes, arrangements function 83
Kierkegaard, Søren 3, 10; authenticity 44; Christiane existentialism 8; *Sickness Unto Death, The* 9
kindness, analyst capacity 96
knowledge, impact 31
Kohut, Heinz 85
Kubrick, Stanley 4

Lacan, Jacques 11, 21, 66; influence 101; short session 65
Laing, R.D. 21, 84; discovery 27–28; *Divided Self, The* 16–17, 28, 100; Heidegger inspiration 19; impact 16–17, 101–103; May, friendship 18; "Philosopher of Madness, The" 17; *Politics of Experience, The* 5, 17; *Politics of the Family, The* 17; *Self and Others* 17, 100; *Voice of Experience, The* 5
Langs, Robert 85
language, function 52
Leavy, Stanley 11, 44, 84
Lefebre, Ludwig 20
Levenson, Edgar 11
Levinas, Immanuel 4
L'existentialisme, popularity 2
lie, overcoming 58
"Lie without a liar" problem 32

life: belief (Aristotle) 57; curveballs 27; history, importance 35; precariousness 64; suffering 56
Lipton, Sam 67, 68, 72, 84
living: non-participation 64; realities (facing), analysis (patient perspective) 56
Loewald, Hans 11, 44, 84, 85
Loewenthal, Del 101
Logotherapy Institutes 17, 20
Lomas, Peter 84
love: impact 63; infantile projections 70; role, emphasis (Freud) 21; role, subtlety 70; transference, equivalence 70

Marcel, Gabriel 2; Christian existentialism 8
Marx, Karl 7
May, Rollo 17, 20, 101; *Existence: A New Dimension in Psychiatry and Psychology* 19; Heidegger inspiration 19; Laing, friendship 18; psychodynamic perspective, adoption 18
meaning, experience (association) 5
Medard Boss Institute (Daseinsanalytic Institute) 17
memory, erasure 65
Menrath, Walter 20
mental distress, relief 58
Merleau-Ponty, Maurice 3, 10, 107; unconscious, examination 31
Middle School (psychoanalysis) 21
Minkowski, Eugène 19
modern/classical technique, Freud technique (difference) 69
moral virtue, standard 53
mother, suicide 14
motivations, knowledge (impossibility) 55
motives, intentional structure (accountability) 37

narcissism 106; impact 52–53, 54
narcissistic patients, analysis possibility (Freud question) 99
Nausea (Sartre) 12
negative transference 69
neuroses, selection 6, 39–40
neurotic, replacement 47
neurotics, suffering 56–57
neurotic symptoms, psychotic symptoms (distinctions) 22
neutrality: feature 60; Freud technical recommendation 11, 58; usage 65
New School for Existential Psychoanalysis (Thompson) 20
New York Psychoanalytic Institute 67
Nietzsche, Friedrich 3; authenticity 44–55; "God is dead" (pronouncement) 8, 46, 54–55; Greeks, impact 10; impact 26; influence 101; Übermensch (overman) conception 46
non-conformity 2
non-conscious 29
non-interpretative communications 91
non-judgmental open-mindedness, analyst capacity 58
non-technical interactions 84
non-transference interactions 84

obsessional neurosis 48, 99, 106
Oceanic experience 47
Oedipus complex, experience 36
opinions, identification 53
Ortega y Gasset, Jose 4
others, experience 50

pain: abolishment 63–64; freedom 64
paranoia 106
passion, sexual feelings (relationship) 35
pathological symptoms 106
paths, difficulty 36

patients: analysts, connection 95; analytic hour control, obsessional attempts 65; experience 95; fantasies, interpretation 30; idealized relationship 72; interpretations, sharing 88; invulnerability abandonment 63–64; one-down position 91–92; suffering, role (reeducation) 57; transference, effect 93
Pearls, Fritz 20
person: censor 31; demise 81; persona, term (invocation) 90; role, examination 82
personal integrity, aspect (abandonment) 47
personality: influence 96–97; traits, confusion 84
personal reactions 92
personal relationship: criteria 72–73; deconstruction 81–93; distinctions 97; foundation 88; recognition (Freud) 69; spontaneity/unpredictability/authenticity 95–96
personal virtue, concept 100
phenomenology 9; origins 9
Philadelphia Association (Laing) 17
"Philosopher of Madness, The" (Laing) 17
philosophy: abstraction, philosophers (opposition) 3; passion, connection 15–16
Picasso, Pablo 4
Plato: authenticity, notion 48; influence 101–102
Politics of Experience, The (Laing) 5, 17
Politics of the Family, The (Laing) 17
Pollock, Jackson 4
positive transference 69
post-traumatic stress disorder (PTSD), presence 106

preconscious 29
projection 75
psychic agency, complexity (determination) 32
psychic conflict 29
psychic reality: conception (Freud) 29–30; factual reality, contrast 29
psychoanalysis: approach 9; conducting 11; creation (Freud) 1; critiques 100–101; cultural divide 44–45; depiction (Freud) 31; elasticity 2; embracing 55–56; existential conception 88; existentialism, relationship 26; goal 43–44; hostility 17–18; marginalization, psychiatry (impact) 55–56; Middle School 21; non-personal elements 82; non-psychoanalytic therapies, distinctions 20–21; personal engagement 20–21; person, demise 81; purpose 64; relational psychoanalysis, development 30; transformation 29; vision (Lacan) 65
Psychoanalysis and Daseinanalysis (Binswanger) 19
psychoanalytic discourse, themes 43
psychoanalytic experience, authenticity/suffering (relationship) 62–66
psychoanalytic interpretation 35
psychoanalytic nomenclature/principles, adoption 101
psychoanalytic practice, components 58
psychoanalytic process, reduction 83
psychoanalytic psychotherapy 88
psychoanalytic relationship, depersonalization 84
psychoanalytic theory, historical evolution 85

psychoanalytic therapist, impact 83
psychoanalytic treatment relationship, context 82
psychoanalytic vocabulary, distinctions 32
psychobabble, rhetoric 58
psychodynamic perspective (May), Yalom adoption 18
psychodynamic therapy 88
psychology, study 16
psychopathology 30; treatment, alternative 22
psychosis 106
psychotherapy: empirical outcomes 107–108; person-based form 82; ploy 6

radical self-acceptance 40–41
Rank, Otto 1
Rat Man, Freud treatment 67–68
real relationship, distinction 92
reflective experience 29
reflective function, discussion 39
Regents College, degree program 17
regression 74
Reik, Theodor 84
relational psychoanalysis, development 30
relational psychoanalysts, distortions perspective 85
Resnais, Alain 4
Ricoeur, Paul: psychoanalysis, examination 31
Rousseau, Jean-Jacques (tangible self conception) 48

sadness, knowledge (absence) 33–34
San Francisco, superficiality 16
San Juan de la Cruz, depiction 8
Sartre, Jean-Paul 8, 10, 14, 23; bad faith 31; *Being and Nothingness* 2, 4, 26, 28; emotions, critique 34–37; formulations, Freud formulations (difference) 34;

freedom, conception 29; Freud, relationship 28; impact 26, 202; inauthenticity 31; *Nausea* 12; non-conformism 27; phenomenological study, purpose 37; philosophy 107; psychoanalysis, relationship 26–27; *Sketch for a Theory of the Emotions* 12, 37; topographical model rejection 31; unconscious: critique 31–34; examination 31
Scheler, Max 10
schizoid patients, analysis possibility (Freud question) 99
schizoid phenomena, study 100
schizophrenia, study 100
Schneider, Kirk 17, 20, 101
second consciousness, model 31
self (selves): authorship 50; construction 50; feeling-states 48–49; freedom 39; narrativist perspective 52; problem 48–49; relationship, standard (need) 53–54; theory, partiality 48
Self and Others (Laing) 17, 100
self-definitions, corruptions fallacy (detection) 52–53
self-disclosure: advocacy, avoidance 93; definition 94; patient acts 58
self-doubt 15
self-exposure, risk 60
self-identity: language, power 51–52; living 8–9
self-knowledge, derivation 48
semi-consciousness, episodic states 51
sex, obsession (Freud) 28
sexual feelings, passion (relationship) 35
sexuality, emphasis (Freud) 1
short session (Lacan) 65
Sickness Unto Death, The (Kierkegaard) 9

Sketch for a Theory of the Emotions (Sartre) 12, 37
social mores, acceptability 53
social relationships, nature 47
social world, theory of intersubjectivity (Sartre application) 32–33
society, Nietzsche rejection 46
Socrates 9; authenticity, notion 48; dialogues 15; execution 10; existentialism 10
Sophists 9
specifically existential dimension 94–97
Spinelli, Ernesto 17, 20, 101
spontaneous conversations, impact 96
Stone, Leo 84, 85
stories: open-ended quality 52; telling, language (function) 52
Strachey, James 85
Stranger, The (Camus) 4
Studies on Hysteria (Freud) 63
subject (self), depiction (distinction) 50
subjectivity 32
subjects, subjectivity 32
suffering: avoidance 62; burden, capacity 62; diminishment, desire 56; fear 63–64; pathogenic form 64; psychoanalytic experience, relationship 62–66; quota, enduring 58; relief, analysis (impact) 58; role, patient reeducation 57
Sullivan, Harry Stack 11, 18, 73
superego: conception (Freud) 63; knowledge 31; language 89
Superman 39
surroundings, totality 49–50
suspended attentiveness 60
symptoms, empirical causes (establishment) 89
synthetic totality 38

tangible self conception, reliance (Rousseau/Descartes) 48
technical interventions (Freud) 68–69; rejection 91
technically-correct instrumentality 72
technical principles, indispensability 98
theory of intersubjectivity, application 32–33
therapeutic alliance 71–72; concept, usefulness 73
therapeutic ambition (Freud) 60
therapeutic process: conception, exclusion 69; enhancement 94
therapeutic situation 38
therapy: pain 61; passion 15–16
things, potentialities (relationship) 36
Thompson, Clara 11
Thompson, Jim 4
Thompson, M. Guy: *Death of Desire: an Existential Study in Sanity and Madness* 22, 82; *Ethic of Honesty, The* 102; *Truth About Freud's Technique, The* 102
Three Essays on the Theory of Sexuality (Freud) 12
Tillich, Paul 4; Christian existentialism 8
topographical model (Freud) 89; replacement 31–32; Sartre rejection 31
totality of surroundings 49–50
total psychotherapeutic encounter 84
transference: concept 75; concept, embracing 89–90; conception (Freud) 63, 90; conception, incompatibility 88–89; countertransference, relationship 45, 66; defense vehicle 72; expansion 70–71; experience, construct 90; extra-transference relationship 45; idea, implication 90; impersonal conception, maintenance 91; love, equivalence 70; nature, insights (Bion) 65; personal nature, elimination 92–93; phenomena, distortions 85; phenomena, psychoanalytic conception 91; psychoanalytic conception, rejection 22; relationship, distinctions 97; relationship, recognition (Freud) 69; technical recommendation (Freud) 11; types 69
transference-countertransference relationship, authenticity (link) 66–75
transference/countertransference situation, usage 72
trauma, presence 106
treatment, goals 43
true artist, feature 47–48
Truffaut, Francois 4
Truth About Freud's Technique (Thompson) 102
truth, impact 31
two-person psychology, advocacy 84

Übermensch (overman), conception (Nietzsche) 46
unconscious: conception (Freud) 29; conception (Freud), dilemma 32; critique (Sartre) 31–34; forces 92; impediments 92; impersonal aspects 30; processes 91; processes, existential therapy rejection 22; psychoanalytic conception 21; second subject 21; theory (Freud) 29; topographical model (Freud) 29
unconscious ideation 91
understanding, impact 31
unhappiness: hysterical misery, impact 63; symptoms 106
universal values, absence 54–55
unobjectionable transference 69

van Deurzen, Emmy 17, 20, 101
Vietnam War 14–15, 27; problems 15; return 15
virtue: idea 53–54; utilitarian aims 57
virtuous character traits, perspective (Freud) 98–99
Voice of Experience, The (Laing) 5

Warhol, Andy 4
Western thought, impact 56
Will, Jr., Otto Allen 11

Winnicott, D.W. 11, 21, 43, 60–61, 63–66, 74, 84
wisdom, analyst capacity 96
words, usage 51–52
working alliance, attention (devotion) 72
world: being-with 49–50; change, attempt 36; perception, change 37
Wright, Richard 4

Yalom, Irvin 17–18, 20; psychodynamic perspective adoption 18